Sociological Foundation of Education

Edited & Complied by:
DR. DEEPESH CHANDRA PRASAD
Ph.D. (Psychology)

KSK Publishers & Distributors
7/26, Basement, Ansari Road, Daryaganj,
New Delhi-110002

Published by:

KSK Publishers & Distributors

7/26, Basement, Ansari Road, Daryaganj,
New Delhi-110002

ISBN: 978-81-903668-2-3

PRINTED IN INDIA 2008

RE-PRINTED IN INDIA 2026

Typeset by:
K.S.K. DTP UNIT, DELHI

Printed at:
ASIAN OFFSET, DELHI

Price: Rs. 800/-

CONTENTS

Chapter 1

Educational Sociology

The distance education is analyzed as a problematic conception in social reality. Because of the educational facts, it has been realized many radical changes in modern era that could be rated as revaluation. New technologies develop continuously distance education models, so it must be expected new revolutions become reality. However, rapid change in social reality causes to lose structural balances and to prevent benefits of distance education.

Since social facts are the subject of sociology, and distance education with its new technologies is being observed in social reality as a very important factor that affects social structure and social change, there shall be a sociological analysis for distance education. In this essay, the phrases of "distance" and "education" are going to be inspected by applying the concepts of social structure and social change as named sociology. At this point, a basic question arises: How does distance education function and change in a given society, if it is taken as a social phenomenon? To make an analysis for the question in this limited work, I am going to use the content analysis and observation methods to examine the terms of distance and education effected by technology with the aspects of social structure and social change. For this aim and as a part of methodology, a point of view must be constructed in order to discuss the distance education with some sociological perspectives and concepts.

In the following parts of this study, some literature is reviewing on the sociology of education. Sociological perspectives are discussed, and then some hypotheses are assumed that taken for granted in this paper. Those analyses have been developed and dealt with them as a sociological problem in distance education such as group structure, social control in society and technological effects on social change. In conclusion, the distance education is examined as a factor that determines social structure. It has primary contribution to social structure. Thanks to distance education methods, necessary knowledge is to diffuse to the person at the forest rank of social structure, and to draw them rapidly to higher ranks. These conclusions are considering that distance education based on technology modifies social reality. However, during this rapid evaluation, the balances in social structure are being loosed, and therefore many social problems arise. Then, new developments of distance education bring up solutions for those problems. Sociological researches in the field of distance education will give some light for the reconstruction of social balances in this circle.

Sociology

Social structure and social change are two proper concepts in the field of sociology to begin any sociological analysis as starting points for sociologists. Therefore, we shall handle distance education with those concepts. Society, as a whole construction, has two aspects that composed of different constituent to function separately and to work together. The concept of "social structure" explains one aspect of society; the components of society and the relationships between each other to construct society together. The "social change" is another aspect of society; at the same time, mean that the society is enrolled in a changing process for a time. We do not encounter any unchanging or fixed society in the history. All institutions, values or social functions are changing at various speeds and ways; they are getting new meanings that are examined by the concept of social change. Every certain form of a social construction or a change in society has influential reasons that are created by them such as social events or scientific discoveries of new educational ways. Therefore, distance education shall be analyzed in the frame of social structural and social change concepts.

Generally, sociology is to examine people's social behavior. Its main idea relating to our subject (the distance education) is that the behaviors are formed by interactions among individuals. In another word, a person's thoughts or acts are effected by his groups. These interactions may go beyond time and space boundaries. The people who live in different time or place are interacting with each other via technology and educational systems. Cultural components spread out distant places and time. The cultural components are transferred by technology to new generations or distant place. A new component may be seen in more than one society at the same time. Similar social facts may be seen in different social groups that are no direct relationships established. The transformation of social values to new generation is also one of them. Different societies have found same set of solutions to organize their needs and to rule their order. Main institutions (such as education, religion, and family) that are created through time can be seen everywhere. Historical observations lead us to the findings that interactions among people have common results. Shortly, continuity of society has been obtained with this interaction, and distance education is one of the tools of society.

Sociology of Education

Some educational researches already have being done by the sociology of education. Essentially, the educational sociology, a sociological field considering distance education in general, and as a branch of applied sociology in particular, has examined educational facts, since at the beginning of this century. Its guiding assumption has been that education is another name for socialization in the broadest sense and should yield rational educational aims and methods and a body of techniques for society. Sociology of education is the application of sociological theories, perspectives and research methods to analyze educational processes and practices (Jary, 1991, p. 472-3). The process of education, on the other hand, has been understood as a contribution to the promotion and maintenance of the social order. Especially, Durkheim and Mannheim's works have been done with the view of functionalism and to regard education as a means of solving problems and removing social antagonisms.

Early studies of this field explain their aim cited from J. Floud that "educational sociology is interested in the impact of the total cultural milieu in which and through which experience is acquired and organized. Educational sociology is particularly interested in finding out how to manipulate the educational process (social control) to achieve better personality development"

It has also been remarked of that "educational sociology included anything in the field of sociology which could be related to the learning or socializing process and anything in education that was subject to sociological analysis". Since then "the sociology of education is concerned with any instruction or training of individuals for which social provision is made, whether or not it is concentrated in the early years of life, undertaken through the agency of specialized institutions, directed generally to the promotion of consensus and integration through the inculcation of attitudes and values or the formation of personality, or specifically to vocational training. In short, its subject-matter is the assimilation of the individuals into a cultural tradition".

In early studies of distance education is not taken as an important subject in the field of sociology of education. It is observed that the importance of the subject has been increased by using technological tools. Today, it is defined as the most industrialized form of teaching and learning and as such also as a typical product of industrial society. Therefore, it seems an educational way of the future.

Sociological Perspectives on Distance Education

There are two main perspectives in sociology to examine social facts. Those are macro-structural and micro-interpretive perspectives. Other perspectives may be included into one of those. Macro perspective assumes that the reasons of variables lie under social structure of social system. Micro perspective stresses more likely social psychological explanations. Both of their dependent variables are the same. Distance education should be examined separately according to those perspectives. To make a sociological analysis we have to clarify and narrow down our perspectives, and suppose assumptions used in this chaper.

More specifically, social researches in sociology should attempt to explain how social groups are formed and shape individuals in the case of distance education. How this process goes on and how is effected by distance education must be questioned in order to begin the explanations. The clearest answer for this question is social mobility. People may exceed time and space, and may not only go easily into any group via educational technology but also create them. Thus, social mobility increases speedily. Depending on this, social reality is changing rapidly, too.

Distance education and technology are contributing to this general fact. Interactions between people and society make education institutionalized and develop technology. The most important factor in new knowledge society is to use new technologies in education. It speeds up the process of social mobility, and condenses socialization. In conclusion, researches in the field of distance education should cover all social units in which socialization is in question.

Distance education is based on technology, so the two main concepts that must be examined are education and technology. Therefore, the first perspective is the relationship between education and technology. In this frame, new problems arise that depend on them. They must be evaluated while we practice them, and the analysis to be done concerning distance education in this paper must be critical. The second perspective is an interaction between individual and society. Furthermore, separated discussions must be done from the angle of individual and society. It must be questioned how distance education is effected from these factors, and what the reasons are for them, and what the direction of change is. Looking for answer for those questions is to frame a perspective.

In this paper, some variables are assumed. The distance education had been granted as explanatory (independent) variable and evaluated its effects on education (therefore social structure) "negativistic" and "skeptically". It means to be the best critic we can be and not accept a particular conclusion until we have examined every possible alternative and been able to discount or discredit them all as much as possible.

However, it cannot be expected to examine deeply every aspect of the distance education in this limited spaces, but we do not phrase our claim in such a way as to make it non falsifiable.

In this frame, our first assumption is that a direct relationship has been constructed with technology and distance education; the changes in social reality are speeded up due to distance education technologies. The effect of "speeding up gradually" is the main premise we shall take into consideration. Therefore, we should not limit the analysis of given methods of distance education. The meanings of distance educational concept will change as technology develops.

Another assumption is that distance education occurs in the remote places through technology. Furthermore, diffusion of knowledge has been gotten under control by using same technological tools. Although, technology makes easy to attain the knowledge, it provides to control the knowledge.

Sociology and Education

Group Structure, Control and Technological Effects in Distance Education

In particular, some matters of distance education should be evaluated with stressing interaction between individual, society, and technology. Those subjects could be classified the group as a unit of social analysis, the control of society as a function of education, and the technology as a determinant both of them.

The first matter in this analysis we evaluate is that the participants of distance education constitute a social group. They are gathering round certain aims. Being together is enough condition for talking about group concept in sociology. However, it should be discussed what kind of groups and groups' effects we are talking about. Distance education is usually defined as not a face-to-face educational way; but this is quite old definition. New technologies give opportunity to people to see their faces even they are not in the same room. Not all members of the group share same actual residence. Students and teachers are not in same place. Their group is imaginary, therefore it has different construction. Direct communication is not supplied. The communication has been established by way of technological tools. Then, many components never have been produced or transferred since the limitation of technology. Some behaviors of people's in-groups are limited. In reality, participants are alone in this kind of group. Whereas, some researches in social psychology show those together actions are more advantageous than single action. The members of face to face group actions encourage each other just because of being same place (Stang, 1981, p. 302-306). The performance of individual is increased if any person watches him. However, it is possible for individual to be discouraged by being under group pressure. The free will and capabilities of individual can not be reflected to his behavior because of group effects. Any natural surroundings created by himself should be the best place to act freely.

The second matter is that educational control has not been constructed formally yet. The problem of not being together in the same residence makes very hard to control the people. Therefore, separated behaviors and attitudes may be developed. For example, there would be no formal clothes to signalize political thoughts.

On the other hand, it largely would not be possible to classify people according to their attitudes and to transform them some information. Emphasizing an institutional ideology is disappeared in this case. It is possible to think the contrary of this case. Such as the national education of European Turkish population could be achieved by using distance education models.

The disappearing of distance gives some opportunities to people in order to choose any cultural norms according to their will. This very important factor provides democracy to spread out. "In distance education it has always been necessary that learners take over responsibilities for their own learning a function which in other circumstances rests with the teacher or the teaching. The learner, therefore, is given the opportunity to develop self-determination, self-direction and self-control to a high degree. They determine where, when, and how long they want to engage themselves in the learning process. If distance education also comprises contract learning the student is also able to determine or to determine what he or she wishes to learn and how to control and evaluate the results of his learning". In conclusion, it is possible to realize socialization based on larger cultural foundation.

The third matter is that the distance education is based on technology. Technological changes determine directly the educational effects on social structure. It not only affects social institutions, but also regulates, and reorganizes their functions. For example, spreading out information networks increases the educated population in the whole world and cumulative amounts of knowledge in varieties. In other words, the crowd of people and the knowledge has increased. The interaction circle between people and knowledge speeds up technological developments, and draws new dimensions in education. For this reason, educational system explanations in social reality vary in bodily structure or function.

Social Change and Distance Education

Above, we had talked about diffusion of social factors through time and space. Social reality is composed by these accumulated components as a meaningful unit. Due to distance educational technology, social reality is changing rapidly. This speed causes many problems, especially in developing countries. New classes or ranks emerge, and society has been faced with new problems like urbanization or industrialization.

How distance education changes social reality is clearly shown by Gouldner's works. He points out the big change in which transformation of knowledge delivers to distance people, in written forms. Structural changes in education create a new class. The distance educational system becomes a major cosmopolitanizing influence on its participants, with a corresponding distancing from localistic interest and values. This development (Gouldner named it as 'situation-freeness') is heightened by the 'communications revolution' in general, and by the development of printing technology, in particular. "With the spread of printed materials, definitions of social reality available to intellectuals may now derive increasingly from distant persons, from groups geographically, culturally, and historically distant and even from dead persons, and may therefore diverge greatly from any local environment in which they are received. Definitions of social reality made by local élites may now be invidiously contrasted (by intellectuals) with definitions made in other places and times," (Gouldner, 1979, p. 3-4). Thus, social reality will develop without the lack of negative effects of given structure. Gouldner sees the factor of distance as one of the basic changes in social structure. Currently, the concept of distance in this meaning has been changed greatly. Well then, anybody reaches immediately any kind of knowledge or sends it anywhere in the world. Time and space boundaries to reach knowledge disappear because of the technology. On the other hand, distance education removes the negative effects of remoteness, too. Losing time, negative controls on the behavior and attitude, expenses, and some handicaps of education are becoming decreased. In conclusion, if we take the knowledge as a component of social reality, we may conclude that the production and diffusion of knowledge (independent variable) effect directly social structure (dependent variable).

At this point, the question of "what kind of knowledge is spreading out?" becomes important, because social structure is changing according to cultures transformed from anywhere. Some people, who catch the information sources by themselves, determine the sort of knowledge to transfer. We are facing more clearly with the problem, which is going to be dealt ahead. An educational system, which is constructed according to the knowledge resources, provides to continue or develop given structure. Therefore some negative components also continue or new problems arise in social reality. Nevertheless, human factor is most efficient components; it should be to take into accounts to solve problems.

Some Functions of Education

The function of education, in general, obtains social mobility as independently from social origins. Educational fact is a kind of relationship between individual and his aim. The goals of individual or society are realizing via education. This relationship is examined by using three explanation systems. Those are determinist, demystifying, and voluntarist explanations. If distance educational models are accepted as models that transfer and transform society, then it must be evaluated with those explanatory systems.

Determinist explanations have two assumptions or two separate determinants, which effect individuals. First, determinist explanation assumes that people are differed from each other intelligently; therefore, the aims are differentiated too. In this case, the distance educational system should be organized according to private peculiarities. Distance educational technology provides us a big rank of possibilities choosing best tools and fitting for any kind of personal peculiarities. All abilities can be classified more easily and knowledge transfer can be delivered in the way that is more suitable. The second determinant is the society itself. People's social classes or statues determine the goals. The successfulness or unsuccessfulness depends completely on personal peculiarities. In this case, the social groups (or class, which individuals belong to it) are more powerful than educational institutions. Some kind of social conditions such as educational tools are social determinants. Therefore, achievements of people depend on given social conditions. The distance education as a developed model may break those negatively determined conditions of society.

Demystifying explanations assumes that the educational institutes are not independent places, and social determinants affect them. In this case, all peculiarities of group are absorbed by distance educational institutions. Therefore, the institutional qualifications reflect people's professions. In other words, some class characters can be observed in people's professions. An individual who reaches to the end of education is shaped according to his groups' differences. "In general, says demystifying sociologist, schools are not 'neutral' social locations, helpless in the face of 'external' social determinations. Their own institutionally embedded practices shape outcomes differentiated by class, gender and other irrelevant discriminators, such as ethnicity". Let us remember distance educational opportunities. Moreover, we can say that it will be very productive for our society if new educational models could remove social determinants.

Voluntary explanations differ from the other systems. This system assumes that a person builds up and prefers his future actively and individually, while others emphasize people's passivity. People are influenced by their social rank, but their perceptions in occupational preferences are more effectual. He may accept or reject the set of values offered in educational institutions. These attitudes depend on his free will and his social orientation. The distance education may increase his alternatives. It can be offered to him some sets of value system including his own. It depends on his private selections. His social origins are not so much important any more. On the other hand, it would be easier to realize them if he prefers a value system suitable to his origin.

In conclusion, the distance education seems very important factor to affect social reality. It is an educational model of the future created by social reality. Social reality is also effected by fast changing technology. Every society has its unique social structure, and therefore effects of distance education depend on those structural components. Building up new structures determines new educational models to transfer given culture to all social ranks and new generations. Consequently, sociological researches about distance education based on cultural (or structural) differences should be done, because it may be seen reflections of social reality.

Distance education could attract people who wish to improve their vocational or professional status as well as their income, sacrificing their leisure time for gratification often delayed for many years.

On the other hands, the traditional models of distance teaching will no longer satisfy the new needs of new types of person with their particular expectations and values which are in many cases even the opposites them. In near future, it is going to be designed new models of distance education. "They will probably be combinations of intensified and sustained group work highly sophisticated ways of acquiring the necessary information for self-study and increased telecommunication between the participants. They will have different sets of goals and objectives. And they will have to rely on self-directing and self-controlling that is, on becoming autonomous students". This is an optimistic point of view. But we should see another site of reality. The problem we are going to face is that social balances are going to be loosed because of very fast social change caused by distance education. Needed structural and institutional conditions are not provided due to speed of technology.

Chapter 2

Social Interactions & its Educational Implications

Social change is a general term which refers to:

- change in the nature, the social institutions, the social behaviour or the social relations of a society or community of people.
- acts of advocacy for the cause of changing society in a positive way.

The term is used in the study of history, economies and politics, and includes topics such as the success or failure of different political systems, globalization, democratization, development and economic growth. The term can encompass concepts as broad as revolution and paradigm shift, to narrow changes such as a particular cause within small town government.

Social change could be:

- slow, gradual, incremental, and evolutionary; in this it might be barely noticeable
- fast, radical, sudden and revolutionary; it might even take people by surprise.
- wide in scope, affecting almost all people in a society
- limited in scope, affecting only a small number of people.

Social change is a topic in sociology, but also involves political science, economics, history, anthropology and many other social sciences.

Theories

Some social change is almost always occurring, but many different theories have been mooted to explain significant social changes in history. These include:

1. the idea of decline or degeneration, or, in religious terms, the fall from an original state of grace, connected with theology;
2. the idea of cyclical change, a pattern of subsequent and recurring phases of growth and decline, and the social cycles;
3. the idea of continuous social progress;
4. Marx's historical materialism
5. Evolutionary theories (how one social form evolves into another), including social darwinism
6. Theories of sociobiology

Examples

Some recent trends in global change are that the world population has become more concentrated in the less developed world and in cities, there has been a tremendous growth in internet use, infant mortality rates have declined, illiteracy has declined, more people are living in freedom, GDP per capita has increased, and poverty has declined.

Measuring social change

These changes did not happen equally throughout the world, however. For example, in 1960, infant mortality rates were more than 4.5 times higher in developing countries than it was among industrialized countries. In 2000, infant mortality rates in developing countries was about 10 times higher than was IMR in industrialized countries. That is, infant mortality rates declined faster among the more developed countries. There were similar disparities in illiteracy and political freedom. That is, conditions did improve among less developed countries, but not as much as they did among more developed countries. In addition, some countries experienced worsening of conditions, for example, increases in infant mortality rates, increases in illiteracy and less freedom.

Social change and social order

The concept of social change contrasts with the concept of social order. Social order is maintained by social institutions and social practices which conserve and enforce "normal" ways of relating. Thus, social change usually means that some or all social institutions are changed, or disappear or are destroyed - depending on how big the social change is. By implication, ways of relating which are considered normal may be considered abnormal later, or vice versa.

Social relation can refer to a multitude of social interactions, regulated by social norms, between two or more people, with each having a social position and performing a social role. In sociological hierarchy, social relation is more advanced then behavior, action, social behavior, social action, social contact and social interaction. Social relations form the basis of concepts such as social organisation, social structure, social movement and social system.

Specific meaning

Although Harvard University has featured a "Department of Social Relations" (in which Talcott Parsons played a prominent role), and although the term "social relations" is frequently used in social sciences, there is in fact no commonly agreed meaning for this concept. "Social" connotes association, co-operation, mutual dependence and belonging.

It could be argued that a social relation is, in the first instance, simply a relation between people, but more specifically

- a relation between individuals insofar as they belong to a group,
- a relation between groups of people, or
- a relation between an individual and a group of people.

The group could be an ethnic or kinship group, a social institution or organisation, a social class or social stratum, a nation, a population, or a gender etc. This definition contrasts with the relationship between people and inanimate objects.

Examples

In this sense, a social relation is therefore not necessarily identical with a unique interpersonal relation or a unique individual relation of some type, although all these kinds of relations presuppose each other; a social relation refers precisely to a condition which groups of people have in common or share.

For example, the simple statement "Jack and Jill love each other" might refer to a unique interaction between two people, the meaning of which might be difficult to define for an outsider. Yet, Jack and Jill may also be socially related in many different ways, insofar as they both are, as a matter of fact, members of the same or different social groups, and thus their identity is shaped in good part by the fact that they belong to those groups. If we wanted to understand and explain their behaviour, we would need to refer to those social relations. We might establish the milieu they grew up in, their ancestors, the jobs they do, where they lived, who their friends are, and so on, all of which helps explain why they necessarily interact in the way that they do, and not in some other way.

At a higher level of abstraction, we might consider two groups which are socially related, for example, although they live in different places, they depend on each other in trading goods and services.

At an even higher level of abstraction, we might consider the relationship between an individual and the whole of the world population, or the relationship of the world population to itself.

Some might indeed argue that a social relation exists between mortals and God (or the Gods), though others would regard this more as an imaginary relation. In flights of fancy, we could extend the analysis to the relation of all sentient organisms in the universe.

Theorists

However, the difficulties only start here, because now it needs to be established how these social relations exist, how we know they exist, what kinds of social relations there are, and how we can find out about them, verify them or identify them. About these questions researchers often disagree and debate, proposing different kinds of methodology to obtain knowledge of social relations.

At one end of the spectrum, Karl Marx approvingly quotes Giambattista Vico's argument that humans can understand their society in its totality because "they made it themselves"; the limits to what humans can know are mainly practical in nature. At the other end of the spectrum, Karl Popper rejects the possibility of objective knowledge about society as a whole, suggesting that methodological holism must lead to totalitarianism; progressive social change can only be achieved through the small steps of piecemeal social engineering.

Understanding social relations

There are at least three problems in understanding social relations.

- many social relations are not directly observable by an individual, and can only be inferred with the aid of abstractions. This raises the question of how we know they exist, and how they exist.
- reflexivity: in the case of social science, the scientist is in a very obvious way himself or herself part of the social world being studied (this occurs also in natural sciences; not just in the sense that a biologist is also a biological being, but also even in theoretical physics - cf. the reflections of David Bohm).
- animal and insect populations for example also display a kind of "social" behaviour, so that social relations are not necessarily uniquely human relations (cf. the insights of sociobiology), and social relations might exist between humans and animals (though some dispute this; they argue that associative relations are confused here with true social relations; a human being could associate with all sorts of things or organisms, without a social relation being involved).

Types of social relations

In broad terms, we can distinguish six basic levels of human awareness:

- sub-conscious awareness (studied by e.g. Sigmund Freud, Carl Jung, and Milton Erickson).
- conscious subjective awareness (dissociated, focusing inward on the inner world, or expressing an inner state outwards) (studied e.g. in phenomenology and general psychology).
- intersubjective awareness (an awareness which occurs in association with other people and is

internal to that association) (studied e.g. in social psychology and sociology).

- objective awareness (dissociated, focusing outward to a world that exists mind-independently, as is developed e.g. in science to a high level).
- reality-transforming awareness (transitions in practical action reframing the boundaries of different forms of awareness and changing consciousness, or connecting different forms of awareness - occurring in work, play, love, activism, politics etc.
- transcendent awareness (going beyond personal knowledge or experience - some would include intuition and spirituality under this heading; it is the subject of much writing in religion and New Age thought).
- Corresponding to these levels of human awareness, we could also define different kinds of social relations, i.e. the different ways in which humans might experience the connections among their own kind:
- subconscious social relations (for example at the level of the collective unconscious or between parents and children,
- social relations which exist only in subjective awareness or subjective perceptions (a person might act as though a social relation exists),
- inter-subjective social relations involving shared meanings conveyed through communication,
- objective social relations which exist whether someone is aware of them or not (they might nevertheless be communicated insofar as we communicate with everything we are and do);
- social relations in the process of being transformed from one kind into another, or being interrelated with each other;
- spiritual or intuitive social relations of some kind.
- As illustration, we can apply the foregoing to the notion of a group.

- A person might almost out of instinct identify with a group or relate to it;
- s/he might imagine being a member of a group, regardless of whether this is really the case;
- a group might exist only in the form of inter-subjective relations among its members;
- a group might exist as an objective description, or as an objective reality, even regardless of whether one was aware of belonging to it;
- a group might be forming or dissolving, or both at once, and it might be changing its boundaries of inclusion and exclusion, perhaps overlapping with other groups;
- a group might also exist at the level of a common spiritual affinity or identification.

However the group may exist, or be perceived to exist at some level - with the obvious consequences that has for the kinds of social relations involved - it is clear that understanding different kinds of group relations require different methods of inquiry and verification.

Precisely because social relations may be experienced at different levels of awareness, they are not necessarily transparent at all. Indeed, Karl Marx wrote ironically in this respect that "science would be superfluous if the outward appearance and the essence of things directly coincided".

Social movements are a type of group action. They are large informal groupings of individuals and/or organizations focused on specific political or social issues, in other words, on carrying out a social change.

Modern social movements became possible through education (the wider dissemination of literature), and increased mobility of labour due to the industrialisation and urbanisation of 19th century societies. The freedom of expression, education and relative economic independence prevalent in the modern Western culture is responsible for the unprecedented number and scope of various contemporary social movements.

Political science and sociology have developed a variety of theories and empirical research on social movements. For example, some research in political science highlights the relation between popular movements and the formation of new political parties as well as discussing the function of social movements in relation to agenda setting and influence on politics.

Political movements that evolved in late 18th century, like those connected to the French Revolution and Polish Constitution of May 3, 1791 are among the first documented social movements. The labor movement and socialist movement of the late 19th century are seen as the prototypical social movements, leading to the formation of communist and social democratic parties and organisations.

From 1815, Britain after victory in the Napoleonic Wars entered a period of social upheaval and change, caused by returning soldiers and unemployment. This resulted in class struggle in the Peterloo Massacre, the Reform Act of 1832, disputes over the Corn laws. Other European countries, such as France, began to see the emergence of political and social movements in the 19th Century. These social movements, set the background to which Karl Marx attempted to analyse social theory more generally. 1861 saw the beginning of the reform movements in Russia, as the feudal system was abolished. Unions, or Soviets were formed from 1905 as pressure for reform continued, resulting in the collapse of the Russian State at the end of the First World War.

In 1945, Britain after victory in the Second World War entered a period of radical reform and change, as a workers rights social movement dominated politics until the election of Margaret Thatcher in 1979. In the 1970s, women's rights, peace, civil rights and environmental movements emerged, often dubbed New Social Movements. They lead inter alia to the formation of green parties. Some find in the end of the 1990s the emergence of a new global social movement, the anti-globalization movement.

Key processes

Several key processes lie behind the history of social movements. The process of urbanisation, which created large cities, facilitated social interaction between scores of people. It was in cities, where people of similar goals could find each other, gather and organise, that those early social movements first appeared. Similarly, the process of industrialisation which gathered large masses of workers in the same region was responsible for the fact that many of those early social movements addressed matters important to that social class. Many other social movements were created at universities, where the process of mass education brought many people together. With the development of communication technologies, creation and activities of social movements became easier - from printed pamphlets circulating in the 18th century coffeehouses to newspapers and Internet, all those tools became important factors in the growth of the social movements. Finally, the spread of democracy and political rights like the freedom of speech made the creation and functioning of social movements much easier.

Types of social movements

Sociologists distinguish between several types of social movements:

Scope

Reform movements - movements dedicated to changing some norms, usually legal ones. Examples of such a movement would include a trade union with a goal of increasing workers rights, a green movement advocating a set of ecological laws, or a movement supporting introduction of a capital punishment or right to abortion. Some reform movements may advocate a change in custom and moral norms, for example, condemnation of pornography or proliferation of some religion.

The Polish Solidarnośc movement of 1980s was an important factor in the fall of the Soviet Union radical movement - movements dedicated to changing some value systems. Those are usually much larger in scope than the reform movements, Examples would include the American Civil Rights Movement which demanded full civil rights and equality under the law to all Americans, regardless of race, or the Polish Solidarity (Solidarnośc) movement which demanded the transformation of communist political and economy system into democracy and capitalism.

Type of Change

Innovation movement - movements which want to introduce new norms, values, etc. The singularitarianism movement advocating deliberate action to effect and ensure the safety of the technological singularity is an example of an innovation movement.

Conservative movement - movements which want to preserve existing norms, values, etc. The anti-machines 19th century Luddites movement or the modern movement opposing the spread of the genetically modified food are examples of conservative movements.

Target Audience

group-focus movements - focused on affecting groups or society in general, for example, advocating the change of the political system. Most of such groups eventually transform into or join a political party.

individual-focused movements - focused on affecting individuals. Most religious movements would fall under this category. Those movements rarely transform into political parties.

Methods of Work

Mohandas Gandhi created the famous peaceful social movement advocating India independence

peaceful movements - opposed to using violent means. Mentioned American Civil Rights movement, Polish Solidarity movement or Mahatma Gandhi civil disobedience movements would fall into this category

violent movements - various armed resistance movements up to and including terrorist organisations. Examples would include the Palestinian Hezbollah, Basque Euskadi Ta Askatasuna (ETA) or Ireland Provisional Irish Republican Army (IRA) movements.

Old and New

old movements - most of the 19th century movements which recruited their followers from a specific social class (only workers, only peasants, only whites, only aristocrats, only protestants, etc.). They were usually centered around some materialistic goals like improving the life standard of the given social class.

new movements - movements which became dominant from the second half of the 20th century - like the feminist movement, civil rights movement, environmental movement, gay rights movement, peace movement, anti-nuclear movement, anti-globalization movement, etc. Sometimes they are known as postmodernism movements. They are usually centered around a non-materialistic goal.

Dynamic of social movements

Social movements are not eternal. They have a life cycle: they are created, they grow, they achieve successes or failures and eventually, they dissolve and cease to exist.

They are more likely to evolve in the time and place which is friendly to the social movements: hence their evident symbiosis with the 19th century proliferation of ideas like individual rights, freedom of speech and civil disobedience. They are more likely to form in the societies and cultures allowing expression of ideas by individuals - like most of the Western culture, which explains why most social movements exist in United States and Europe, and fewer in more autocratic places like Russia or China. Such friendly context and environment is only a background facilitating the creation of the social movement. There must also be polarizing differences between groups of people: in case of 'old movements', they were the poverty and wealth gaps. In case of the 'new movements', they are more likely to be the differences in customs, ethics and values. Finally, the birth of a social movement needs what sociologist Neil Smelser calls an initiating event: a particular, individual event that will begin a chain reaction of events in the given society leading to the creation of a social movement. For example, American Civil Rights movement grew on the reaction to black women, Rosa Parks, riding in the whites-only section of the bus (although it is important to note that Rosa Parks was not acting alone or spontaneously -- typically activist leaders lay the groundwork behind the scenes of interventions designed to spark a movement). Polish Solidarity movement, which eventually toppled the communist regimes of Eastern Europe, developed after trade union activist Anna Walentynowicz was fired from work. Such an event is also described as a volcanic model - a social movement is often created after a large number of people realise that there are others sharing the same value and desire for a particular social change. Thus, one of the main difficulties facing the emerging social movement is spreading the very knowledge that it exists. Second is overcoming the free rider problem - convincing people to join it, instead of following the mentality 'why should I trouble myself when others can do it and I can just reap the benefits after their hard work'.

Incident of Rosa Parks who was arrested for refusing to give up her seat to make room for white people sparked the American Civil Rights Movement

Many social movements are created around some charismatic leader, i.e. one possessing charismatic authority. After the social movement is created, there are two likely phases of recruitment. The first phase will gather the people deeply interested in the primary goal and ideal of the movement. The second phase, which will usually come after the given movement had some successes and its fame increased, will gather people whose primary interest lie in joining the movement for 'being in it' - because it's trendy; it would look good on a résumé. People who join in this second phase will likely be the first to leave when the movement suffers any setbacks and failures.

Eventually, the social movement will move towards a crisis. If it has achieved its intended goal, then it is called a victory crisis, as most members leave the movement assuming there is no longer any need for its continued existence. This will likely be opposed by a minority of members, for whom the existence of the very movement has become the primary goal itself, and likely the source of their income. Few social movements have survived a victory crisis, often merging with other similar movements or transforming into a tiny, caricatural form of their early selves. Another type of crisis is a failure crisis, which can be seen in increasing demoralisation and disenchantment of members, when they lose faith in the possibility that the primary goal of the movement can be ever achieved. Failure crisis can be encouraged by outside elements, like opposition from government or other movements.

However, many movements had survived a failure crisis, being revived by some hardcore activists even after several decades.

Education for Social Cohesion

Compulsory, standardized, public schooling has traditionally been a central vehicle for the creation and consolidation of a common sense of belonging, identity and social cohesion within the model of the nation-state. Yet, schooling sometimes fails in this essential function, reflecting and even exacerbating existing social and political tensions and conflicts. The efficiency of formal education as an instrument of integration and social cohesion is thus being increasingly called into question as rapid structural changes associated with the multiple processes of globalization weaken traditional models of social, political and economic organization. Concerns with the deterioration of social cohesion are most often related to observed increases in inequalities in income distribution both within and across countries, increasing social exclusion and an apparent rise in the incidence of violence in all societies. Indeed, the combination of socioeconomic disparities, social exclusion, and easily politicized cultural factors such as ethnicity, language, and religion, often lead to violence and to the breakdown of social cohesion. It may be argued that manifestations of physical violence are indicative of the breakdown of social bonds associated with the multiple processes of social exclusion at the cultural, political and economic levels. How do the content and processes of formal education relate to processes of social exclusion and to patterns of violence associated with the breakdown of social cohesion?

After the necessary epistemological clarifications of the terms 'social exclusion' and 'violence', this paper sketches out some ideas relative to the causes and consequences of diverse manifestations of violence from the perspective of their dialectical links with the content and process of education. More specifically, the discussion will be organized around the following clusters of guiding questions :

- What consequences does societal violence have on education ? How much of, and in what ways does societal violence translate into the learning experience in schools ? In what way is societal violence related to school-based violence ?
- To what extent and how does formal education act as a catalyst or precipitating factor in the process of social disintegration and the outbreak of violence ?
- How can education effectively contribute to strengthening or rebuilding social cohesion and to preventing violence at school and in society at large ?

Epistemological issues

Any attempt at identifying and exploring these interrelations, however, requires clear definitions of what is meant by such terms as social exclusion and violence. As a multidimensional notion conceived to capture the various political, social and economic processes of social disadvantage, the notion of social exclusion may be seen as encompassing a series of exclusions that may be economic in nature (exclusion from employment, means of production, land...), political (denial of security, representation, citizenship, rights...), or social (exclusion from education, health services, or housing...). Although the concept of social exclusion clearly overlaps with more conventional conceptual frameworks such as poverty, inequality, and deprivation, educational exclusion is often seen as being central to other processes of exclusion. As far as violence is concerned, a wide definition covers a wide array of human interactions ranging from the use or the threat of the use of force, to armed conflict and even to other forms of denial of human dignity associated with extreme poverty. In addition to the crucial distinction between the overt forms of violence of gangs and armed struggles, and covert forms of structural and symbolic violence, it is necessary to distinguish between patterns of violence at interpersonal and inter-group levels.

Armed conflict and educational exclusion

A significant number of countries in which declining school enrolments were observed during the 1980s were already recognized as being affected by chronic political instability, insecurity and armed conflict. During the past decade of international efforts toward EFA, political violence was progressively recognized as an "emerging challenge" (Amman 1996) and the "needs of (...) children and adults affected by armed conflict" came to figure in the Dakar Framework for Action.

- What proportion of the reported 113,000,000 school-age children who are not enrolled in school reside in areas affected by political violence and armed conflict?
- Are education for all goals attainable given the apparent spread in internal armed conflicts around the world?
- To what extent have educational interventions been successfully integrated into the design of emergency relief responses? What types of partnerships have proved effective in responding to educational needs of populations in conflict-affected areas?

Education as a catalyst for violence

What role does education play as a catalyst to the multiple socio-economic, cultural and political processes that may be associated with the weakening and general breakdown of social cohesion and the outbreak of violence? The growing recognition that education is often a target of political violence, has prompted a greater concern with the ways in which the content and process of education may actually contribute to precipitate the outbreak and development of violent conflict. The Dakar thematic assessment study on education in emergencies (2000) recognized that "weaknesses in education structures and content may have contributed to civil conflict" and that "an education system that reinforces social fissures can represent a dangerous source of conflict".

What case studies have been researched to establish causal links between the content and the processes of education and internal strife?

Education and social exclusion

How does formal education contribute to the multiple social processes of exclusion at the economic, political and cultural levels? Authoritarian education systems, for example, are explicit instruments of political domination and exclusion often based on discrimination and denial of cultural and political rights. However, education systems also contribute to perpetuating economic disparities and inequalities as is illustrated by the continued denial of access to basic education for a significant proportion of children in many regions of the world. The recent shift in focus from supply to demand- side considerations when dealing with the issue of access to basic education, indicates that issues pertaining both to household poverty and to the quality of education have become key to understanding why over 110 million primary school-age children in the developing world continue to be denied access to school. Exclusion from education may be seen as "part of an intricate web of human rights violations" (Dakar 2000), and the widespread and increasing failure of schooling to ensure socio-economic integration of individuals and groups to the labour market, to adequate levels of consumption, for example, questions the efficiency of formal education as an instrument both of redistribution and of upward mobility.

How does the failure of schooling in its integrative and distributive functions contribute to undermine the legitimacy of existing power structures?

School-based violence

Although not new, the phenomenon of school-based violence points to a social problem of increasing importance in countries both in the North and South as is reflected in the increasing media coverage of this complex phenomenon. Physical and symbolic manifestations of school-based violence are multiple and include bullying between youngsters, intimidation and physical aggression towards teaching personnel, vandalism, racketeering, and sexual violence. Any serious attempt to understand this particular category of violence goes well beyond the confines of the school itself to include wider social considerations relative to the strains of economic crisis and transition, cultural alienation and social exclusion. The symbolic and cultural violence of schooling largely reproduce and perpetuate structural inequalities. Learners from minority, immigrant, and other possibly disadvantaged groups are often less-well equipped to adjust to the normative and social demands of school culture that is anchored in middle class values. In this perspective, anti-school violence may be interpreted as a response to the violence of the educational process itself and to the inability of schooling to adapt to changes in the wider social environment. Finally, school-based violence may also be a reflection of violence in wider society, as active or passive participation of youth in domestic and political violence has direct repercussions on their learning experience in school.

- Is not each manifestation of school-based violence different in nature thus calling for differential responses ?

- How do the frustrations of unfulfilled expectations among youth confronted with unemployment, failed cultural integration and disintegration of popular cultures translate into violence at school ?
- To what extent is violence towards school by youth a product of, and a response to, the school experience and the symbolic violence imposed on students belonging to minority and other disadvantaged groups?

Education for Social Cohesion

- While the content and unintended consequences of schooling may act as precipitating factors in the breakdown of social cohesion and in the possible outbreak of violence, formal education also has an important role to play in strengthening or rebuilding social cohesion. Differences must, however, be made between educational systems as victims of social and political violence and the potential role of education in the reproduction of exclusion and social and political violence.
- What successful strategies exist in terms of curriculum design and educational management that overcome the tensions inherent to contradictory aims such as selection and competitiveness versus egalitarianism, standardization versus respect for particularisms, centralization versus decentralization, nation-building versus universalism?
- What conditions are necessary for education systems to minimize, if not prevent, wider social and political tensions?
- How can education contribute to rebuilding social cohesion, particularly in the wake of violent civil conflict and confrontation?
- In the case of school-based violence, measures taken to prevent or reduce the incidence of violence are commonly articulated around information, prevention, and repression. In

addition to the necessary external controls of repressive measures, preventing violence aims to develop a commitment to norms and values imbedded in social networks may inhibit the recourse to violent behaviour.

- To what extent can the schooling system alone be expected to be effective in preventing or reducing the incidence of school-based violence ?
- What successful strategies have been documented in differing contexts of school violence ?
- What types of partnerships have obtained positive results ?

Student Interactions within Cooperative Learning Groups

National calls for reform in education have urged schools to recognize that different students may learn in different ways and an emphasis needs to be placed on how students learn best. There are several methods in which teachers can present material and several ways in which students prefer to learn the material; the learning process is not the same for all students and teachers must acknowledge and act upon these variations. Cooperative learning is one way teachers can recognize differences in students' learning styles.

Cooperative learning is the instructional use of small groups in which students work together to maximize their own and other students' learning. "Whether the groups solve problems, perform open-ended laboratories, give presentations, or prepare for quizzes or exams, discussing information in a group requires students to be more active in their learning". The use of cooperative small groups in instruction allows students to participate more freely and interact with each other while developing greater social skills. Cooperative learning is also linked with greater achievement levels, greater retention of information, higher self-esteem, and enhanced conceptual development across content areas.

As a teaching strategy, cooperative learning is very dependent upon student interactions that occur in the learning environment. These types of interactions serve as predictors for why cooperative learning is successful and it is important to understand these interactions in order to know how cooperative learning results in success. Most previous studies have used quantitative methods to determine the effects of student interactions on achievement, retention, and social skills; however, few studies have examined these interactions qualitatively to specify the types of interactions that occur.

The purpose of this study is to determine: When using cooperative learning methods, what types of interactions take place among seventh-grade students in a Work and Family Studies class?

Definitions

Cooperative Learning:

An instruction method in which students work in groups toward a common academic goal.

Interaction:

Any communication, whether verbal or nonverbal, that occurs between two or more group members.

Literature Review

The literature review begins by analyzing the characteristics and uses of cooperative learning as a teaching method, along with how cooperative learning can also affect students' social learning. The effects of cooperative learning on achievement will then be discussed. Finally, the interactions that occur during cooperative learning will be examined.

Cooperative Learning as a Teaching Strategy

"National advisory committees, researchers, and employers all point toward using small-group learning activities as a method of enhancing achievement and developing 'professional life skills' such as communication and teamwork skills". These small-group learning activities can also be described as cooperative learning, "the generic classroom learning technique which requires students to work and talk together about academic material while learning effective, positive, interpersonal skills". It has been found that students possess different learning styles and cooperative learning is one successful teaching method that can assist instructors in reaching these styles. Recent reviews of cooperative learning show that it leads to positive outcomes such as higher achievement, increased positive attitudes toward the subject area being studied, higher self-esteem, enhanced verbal skills, greater acceptance of differences among peers, greater persistence, greater retention, and enhanced conceptual development across content areas. An additional benefit is the opportunity students receive to work with others.

"A major component of cooperative learning is the development of effective social skills behaviors". There are four major social skills areas, including: trust, communication, leadership, and conflict resolution. While working in groups, students are able to facilitate the development of these social skills, which are imperative for their relationships with others. "Leadership, decision-making, trust-building, communication, and conflict-management skills have to be taught just as purposefully and precisely as academic skills". Fortunately, using cooperative learning as a learning environment will aid the development of both academic and social skills.

"Cooperative group learning refers to the use of small, structured groups of heterogeneous-ability students completing academic tasks together in an interdependent, cooperative environment". Positive interdependence is one of the critical attributes of cooperative learning and it is a term that describes each member's goal attainment as having a positive effect on the goal attainment of other members. The peer relationships formed during cooperative learning can help improve academic performance and have a profound impact on how students feel about school, academic excellence, and studying (Johnson, 1985). During cooperative learning it is imperative that the group members discuss how well they are achieving their goals and maintaining effective working relationships; the interactions between members are helpful in focusing the group on their goals. When implemented correctly, cooperative learning can have a great influence on student achievement.

Cooperative Learning and Achievement

Cooperative learning can be described as a type of social learning and Elias states, "when schools attend systematically to students' social and emotional skills, the academic achievement of children increases". Also, teaching styles that enhance the social development of students usually lead to more effective interaction among students along with a greater understanding of how to successfully manage life's tasks. Social education efforts typically involve more active learning techniques and the generalization of skills across different subject areas while allowing students to work more effectively in a group.

When cooperative learning is implemented in the classroom, students are more likely to acquire critical thinking skills and achieve at a higher level as opposed to listening to lectures. Along with positive effects on student achievement, cooperative learning should also result in an increased retention of information. In a study conducted by Rosini Abu, the effects of cooperative learning on achievement and retention of information were examined in North Carolina home economics students. Two groups of students were formed; cooperative learning methods were used in the instruction of one group while noncooperative methods were used for the other group. The results of the study show that cooperative learning methods are just as effective as noncooperative methods with regard to achievement and retention; in addition, cooperative learning also contributes to the development of interpersonal skills and the ability to work effectively in a group.

Further studies have resulted in more conclusive evidence supporting the claim that cooperative learning increases achievement and helps students develop social skills. One study, conducted by Mollie Landfear and Julie Innis, investigated the relationship between cooperative learning and teamwork skills. During a five-month action research project, a program was developed that implemented cooperative learning in order to improve the teamwork skills of high school home economics students. A survey was completed by the students before and after the program was implemented and participating teachers noticed an increase in the students' understanding of group dynamics and team building. Another study evaluated the effects of cooperative learning on students' verbal interaction patterns and achievement in secondary science. Tenth-grade students received identical content instruction on the particle model of matter; however, an experimental section of students used cooperative learning strategies involving instruction in collaborative skills and group evaluation of assignments. The control group of students received no collaborative skills training and their assignments were evaluated individually. Results from the study illustrate that students using cooperative learning strategies show greater achievement gains and a greater use of specific verbal patterns. Not only did cooperative learning help teach students verbal interaction skills; it also produced an environment that is conducive to the use of these skills.

Cooperative learning is a learning environment that requires a high level of student involvement, and the question might be asked, 'Can it involve all types of learners?' Lorin Anderson performed a study that asked: "Are there types of teaching methods that maximize and minimize differences in involvement among different types of learners Students were observed and ranked according to their aptitude and academic self-concept and it was found that all learners, regardless of their aptitude or self-concept, can be involved in group work. In a related study Bruce Tuckman (1968) hypothesized that, "for vocational and nonvocational teachers, a directive teaching style would be more effective with concrete authoritarian students and a nondirective teaching style would be more effective with abstract, nonauthoritarian students".

Student satisfaction with the course, student relative preference for the teacher, and student grades were analyzed separately for vocational and nonvocational teachers by two factors: teacher directiveness or nondirectiveness and student personality orientation. The findings of the study disproved the hypothesis in that all students were more satisfied with, preferred, and earned high grades from nondirective teachers in both vocational and nonvocational subjects). Cooperative learning, therefore, can benefit student learning.

Lastly, can cooperative learning enhance critical thinking skills? A study by Anuradha Gokhale (1995) examined the relationship between achievement and cooperative learning by administering a test composed of critical-thinking items to both students learning individually and students learning cooperatively. The test scores of the students who learned cooperatively were significantly higher than the test scores of the students who learned on their own (Gokhale, 1995). In this case, cooperative learning did enhance critical thinking skills and students were able to improve their performance by interacting effectively with each other.

Interactions and Achievement

Most of the studies addressed thus far have focused on cooperative learning as a learning environment and its subsequent effects on achievement and social skills. During the process of cooperative learning, however, several interactions take place among students that vary in kind and frequency. How do these student-to-student interactions effect achievement? And, what kinds of interactions take place? These questions will be discussed next.

A primary reason for using cooperative learning in the classroom is the opportunity students have to help each other learn. "Students can learn from other students by giving and receiving help, by recognizing contradictions between their own and other students' perspectives, seeking new knowledge to resolve those contradictions, and constructing new understandings from them". There can generally be three types of group members in the cooperative setting: students who explain, students who receive explanations, and students who may participate in both methods. The process of giving explanations to other students may encourage explainers to clarify or reorganize material along with allowing them to fill in gaps in their own understanding. Students who receive the explanations can also fill in gaps in their understanding, while correcting misconceptions and strengthening connections between new information and previous learning. All of the interactions that take place within the small group may have a direct effect on the students' achievement.

A study conducted by Noreen Webb, Jonathan Troper, and Randy Fall (1995) identified student interactions that best predict mathematics learning in peer-directed small groups among students who need help. The goal of their study was to determine the conditions and interactions necessary for help received to be effective for learning. Six seventh-grade mathematics classes participated in two instructional units during the study and 119 students were identified as needing help with their learning. The results indicate that two main types of interactions predict higher achievement levels among students needing help: receiving explanations instead of less elaborated help and using the explanations received in problem-solving activities. The extent to which students continued working on the problems after receiving explanations was the strongest predictor of achievement, more important than prior achievement or the level of help received.

A similar study investigated sex differences in interaction patterns and achievement in small groups in two junior high school mathematics classes (Webb, 1984). The sample consisted of seventy-seven students who worked for two weeks in majority-female, majority-male, or groups with equal numbers of males and females. Interactions were analyzed among same-sex and cross-sex groups; six interactions were focused on, including giving, asking for, and receiving explanations and giving, asking for, and receiving procedural information. The results show that achievement and interaction are related to the ratio of females to males in a group and to the use of cooperative small groups. Likewise, in a study conducted by Helen Dale (1994) it was found that interactions in a ninth-grade classroom affect the writing skills of students when they work in collaborative small groups. "The most effective collaborative writing discourse occurred among students writing in a positive social environment who were engaged with each other, the writing process, and the topic". Also, the success of these writing groups depend largely on the ability of the students to form social skills within their cooperative group because, "what students write is a product of their social interactions". The types of interactions that take place in a cooperative learning environment do have an affect on the amount of learning that occurs and it is important to discover the specific types of interactions that may occur.

Interactions in Cooperative Learning

Previous studies have shown that cooperative learning has a profound affect on student learning and the social skills students develop while working in groups. One question that deserves to be answered, however, pertains to why cooperative learning can be effective. Few studies have been conducted that examine the group dynamics that occur within cooperative learning; those that have been conducted will be discussed next.

Carla Boxtel, Jos Van Der Linden, and Gellof Kanselaar (1997) conducted an experimental study in which interaction processes and learning outcomes of dyads working on different cooperative tasks were compared. The sample for their study was 40 students, 16-17 years old, who were enrolled in physics classes and experienced at working in cooperative groups. During the study student interactions were recorded on videotapes and transcripts of these tapes were used to describe the nature of the students' verbal interactions through categories. The most frequent types of interactions that occurred were statements, arguments, and questions, particularly verification questions. Another study, conducted by Barak and Maymon (1998), analyzed the different types of teamwork behaviors that occur during a technological task. To accomplish this goal a four-hour workshop was developed in which students from seven schools designed and constructed an envelope for a hot-air balloon from tissue paper. Their degree of involvement in the group and the level of energy they demonstrated in relation to their work measured the motivation of the students and it was found that most students exhibited a high level of motivation. The students displayed other group interactions such as patterns of role assignment, decision-making consensus, and random decisions.

Several different types of interactions have been found to occur within cooperative learning groups and the relationships that exist among these interactions may give insight as to why cooperative learning is effective. Robert Lonning (1993) evaluated the effects of cooperative learning on students' verbal interaction patterns and found that, "students using cooperative learning strategies made greater use of specific verbal patterns believed to be related to increased learning".

Specifically, these verbal patterns consisted of providing help and clarification, acceptance, sharing argument strategies, and requests for help from other students. Another researcher investigated the strengths and interactions within cooperative learning by observing a discussion that took place among ninth graders about world religions. Four students were given fifteen minutes to complete a task and some of the strengths that were highlighted are: all students were engaged in the task, on-task, and attempting to complete their responsibilities. The students were also interacting with each other by contributing to the overall discussion.

Student interactions are an important aspect of cooperative learning and it has been shown that cooperative learning may be effective because of these differing interactions. Few studies have been conducted which focus primarily on the occurring interactions and not on the direct effects of cooperative learning; the aim of this study is to identify the types of interactions that occur among middle school Work and Family Studies students who are engaged in cooperative learning methods.

Procedures

Sample

A convenience sample of two seventh-grade Work and Family Studies classes from a middle school in Virginia will be used for the study. Each class will consist of 25 students and observations will be collected on all students during the research process. Approximately

20% of the students will be male and 80% of the students will be female. The same teacher will teach both classes.

Instrumentation

Data on verbal interaction among group members will come from non-exact transcription of audiotapes of group work. Data on nonverbal interaction among group members will come from field notes recorded by the observer during cooperative group work. These instruments were selected by the researcher to provide the most valid portrayal of the student interactions that occur among seventh graders during cooperative learning in a Work and Family Studies classroom.

Data Collection

Before the study will begin, students will be assigned to small groups according to gender and achievement. The ability of each student will be determined beforehand according to their current course grade. Each group will consist of five members and all five groups will consist of one male and four female members. During the study students will be covering units on food and nutrition, clothing, goals and resources, families and relationships, and child development. Students will work in small groups throughout the study to accomplish tasks such as worksheets, presentations, problem-solving activities, and exams. The teacher will not assign roles to specific students; students will be instructed to work within their group to see what roles may develop.

Each week, dialogue from one group will be recorded for 30 minutes using a micro cassette recorder; by the end of the first ten weeks of the study the researcher will have at least 30 minutes of dialogue from each group in both classes. Each group and each group member will be assigned a number to ensure confidentiality and the researcher will identify each group before their dialogue is recorded. Also, while the verbal interactions are being recorded, the researcher will record field notes on the nonverbal interactions that occur among the group members.

The study will continue for 34 weeks with the researcher continuing to collect weekly group dialogues and field notes on each group. By the end of the study the researcher will have gathered 17 hours of cooperative learning dialogue.

Data Analysis

The non-exact transcription of the audiotapes and the field notes will be analyzed by the researcher to look for themes or patterns within the verbal and nonverbal interactions that occur among students working in cooperative groups. Each theme or pattern will be assigned a code and categories will be developed to group the codes according to the kind of interaction they specify.

Pilot Study

The researcher conducted a pilot study during the week of March 8-15, 2000. One seventh-grade Work and Family Studies classroom was used for the study and five cooperative learning groups were observed. Each group consisted of five members, although only three groups had one male and four female members. Two groups consisted of five female members. The groups were instructed to complete a worksheet on food safety and sanitation using their textbooks, class notes, and each other. They were also instructed not to share answers with other group members and to work together.

The dialogue of each of the five groups was recorded for at least 15 minutes throughout the 90-minute class period using a micro cassette recorder. The groups were also assigned a number and identified by the researcher at the beginning of the taping. The researcher also recorded field notes on the nonverbal interactions that occurred among group members while they were completing the worksheet.

The recordings were transcribed using non-exact transcription and the data was analyzed for themes and patterns that existed among the verbal and nonverbal interactions that occurred among seventh-grade students working in cooperative group settings. Results show that the types of verbal interactions that occurred most frequently were asking for help, explaining concepts, and attempting to keep the group focused and on-task. For example, one group member stated, "Come on you guys, this is for a grade, and we need to get to work". The most frequent types of nonverbal interactions that occurred were students nodding their heads in agreement and expressing looks of confusion to their group members. One change that will be made before the study is conducted is that another participant will record the field notes on nonverbal interactions.

Limitations

One limitation of this study is the use of non-exact transcription when transcribing the audiotapes of students' verbal interactions during cooperative learning. Due to budgetary constraints this limitation cannot be controlled completely by using professional transcription, but the researcher will transcribe the audiotapes as accurately as possible.

Another limitation of this study may be the maturation of the subjects involved in the research. Before the study is begun the students will be placed into small groups based upon their ability, which is determined according to the student's current course grade. During the study, however, students' grades may change several times and this may affect the internal validity of the study. Also, the type of sample that will be used in this study is a convenience sample, which will limit the external generalizability of the findings.

Lastly, another limitation may be mortality in that all five members of each group may not be present for each dialogue taping and nonverbal interaction recording. Also, students may leave and enter the class at any time throughout the year and this may pose difficulties for the researcher to correctly analyze the group interactions.

Designing Effective Group Activities

Over the last few years group activities have become increasingly popular. However, instructors and workshop leaders frequently report three common problems that greatly reduce the effectiveness of small-group based learning activities. Two of the three problems typically occur while students or workshop participants are actually engaged in the group work. Probably the most common problem is that one or two vocal individuals often dominate the discussions to the point that quieter members' ideas are either unexpressed or largely ignored. Alternatively, groups frequently have difficulty staying focused on the assigned task because they get side-tracked on inconsequential or irrelevant details. The third problem occurs when groups are reporting the results of their work to the total class. Even when there has been a high level of engagement in the small groups subsequent whole-class discussions sometimes "fall flat."

Based on our experience, these "problems" are actually symptoms that are almost always the result of poorly conceived group tasks. Further, we believe that all three of these problems can be avoided if classroom teachers and faculty developers use activities that are designed to take into account: 1) the developmental level of the groups in which they will be used and, 2) the impact of the activity on the cohesiveness of the groups.

With this in mind, our primary objective in writing this article is to provide a set of conceptual tools to provide guidance for designing effective group assignments and activities for classes and workshops. Overall, the most important idea in the paper is that the most reliable way to gauge the learning value of group assignments is to examine their impact on group cohesiveness. Accordingly, a second objective in writing this article is to help readers understand how different types of learning tasks contribute to or detract from group cohesion.

In the pages that follow, we:

1. discuss the psychological processes that result in uneven participation by group members;

2. identify four key variables that must be managed in order to create a group environment that is conducive for broad-based member participation and learning;

3. describe the cognitive processes through which learning occurs and discuss the implications for designing effective learning activities;

4. outline the impact of assignment wording on learning and group development;

5. present a checklist for evaluating and/or designing effective group activities in a variety of subject areas and educational settings;

6. Use a "before-after" example of a group assignment from one of our colleague's classes to illustrate why the effectiveness of group activities is so closely tied to their impact on group cohesiveness.

The Nature of Group Interaction

Under certain conditions, a high percentage of group members would prefer to sit back and let "someone else" work on their behalf. This phenomenon, which has come to be known as "social loafing" (Latane, Williams & Harkins, 1979) can be a serious problem in classrooms and workshops because it heavily constrains the interaction necessary for a productive learning environment. Further, if left unchecked, the conditions that produce social loafing can prevent the development of the social fabric that is necessary for effectively functioning learning groups. More assertive members will inevitably "take charge" and, by doing so, will both reduce the need for additional input and create a sort of a "caste" system in which quieter members often feel that their ideas might not be welcomed.

We have identified six forces which, unless recognized and dealt with by the instructor or workshop leader, will produce a level of social loafing that will be a serious problem in most learning groups. Three of these have to do with the characteristics of group members. First, some people are naturally resistant to participation (e.g., shy). Second, others prefer to dominate a discussion. Third, members who feel they lack content knowledge of the task at hand are usually reluctant to speak because they are concerned about being seen as incompetent. Two others are especially problematic in newly formed and/or temporary groups. These are that members of new and/or temporary groups are typically more concerned about their own personal image than that of the group and also see themselves as having little to lose if the group fails to perform effectively. Finally, the group task promotes social loafing when it can be completed by one member working alone and/or doesn't require members to reach an agreement.

The forces that promote social loafing in learning groups, however, can largely be offset by assignments and practices that foster the development of cohesive learning groups. There are two reasons for this. First, as groups become more cohesive, trust and understanding typically build to the point that even naturally quiet members are willing and able to engage in intense give-and-take interactions without having to worry about being offensive or misunderstood. Second, a primary characteristic of cohesive groups is that members see their own well being as being integrally tied to the success of their group. As a result, members of cohesive groups are often highly motivated to invest personal energy doing group work.

Characteristics of Learning Tasks that Promote Group Cohesiveness

The single most effective strategy for eliminating social loafing is to ensure that four key dimensions of the learning tasks cause members to interact in ways that promote the development of cohesive groups. Specifically, the tasks should be explicitly designed to: 1) require a high level of individual accountability for group members and/or workshop participants, 2) motivate a great deal of discussion among group members, 3) ensure that members receive immediate, unambiguous and meaningful feedback (preferably involving direct comparisons with the performance outputs from other groups), and 4) provide explicit rewards for high levels of group performance.

Ensuring individual accountability. Instructors or workshop leaders often inadvertently foster social loafing by failing to ensure that their group assignments (especially the first one) require input from every group member. The initial assignment is key for two reasons. First, the innate forces against broad-based participation in new groups are so powerful that they must be offset early on. Second, if the group is even modestly successful with input from only one or two members,. then it is highly likely that the group will develop a norm supporting at least partial non-participation of members (Feldman, 1984).

On the other hand, if the task explicitly requires input from group members, then the question of whether their input is needed becomes a moot point. As a result, at least two of the negatives are turned into positives. One is that members are faced with the possibility of being seen in a negative light if they don't contribute. The other is that, because of the additional input, the groups are both more likely to succeed, which reinforces a norm that everyone is expected to provide input to the group. These dynamics are two of the main reasons that giving an individual test followed immediately by a group test is such a powerful learning and group-building tool. Another way to ensure broad-based input in small group discussions is to hand out an individual worksheet and ask participants to take a few minutes to think through the issues and write down their ideas prior to the start of the group discussions.

Motivating intensive group interaction. The most common cause of social loafing is the use of assignments that can be completed by independent individual work. When the rational way to complete a task is to "delegate" the work to individual members, that is exactly what will happen. Delegating commonly occurs in two situations. One situation is when the assignments are too easy (i.e., group interaction isn't needed). In this case, one member will simply act on behalf of the group. The other situation occurs when the task requires a great deal of writing. Since writing is inherently an individual activity, the only real group activity will be deciding how to divide up the work. When group members work independently, cohesiveness is reduced for at least two reasons. The first reason is that some members always feel like they are having to do more than their fair share (and in most cases, they probably are correct). The other reason is that, depending on the group's performance, the top students are likely to resent having to choose between carrying their less able or less motivated peers or risk getting a low grade.

Although a number of different types of tasks will reliably produce high levels of group interaction, a highly reliable "rule-of-thumb" is that assignments increase group cohesiveness (and, over time, eliminate social loafing) when they require members to make a concrete decision based on the analysis of a complex issue. In other words, when we ask students or workshop participants to apply a rule or solve a problem. This type of task typically requires students to use a broad range of intellectual skills including: recognizing and defining concepts, making discriminations, and applying principles or procedural rules (Gagne, 1970). Further, everyone typically has both opportunities and incentives to participate actively in completing the task because of the genuine need for broad-based member input. The net result is that problem-based tasks almost universally immerse students and/or workshop participants in an information-rich, give-and-take discussions through which their content learning increases. Further, if the assignment is thoughtfully crafted, they are also likely to learn two important lessons about their group. They are: 1) other members' input is a valuable resource, and 2) we can accomplish something by working together that none of us could have accomplished on our own.

Facilitating external [meaningful] performance feedback. The single most powerful force for the development of group cohesiveness is the presence of an outside influence that is perceived to be threatening to member goals and/or the well-being of the group (Shaw, 1981). Differences among members become less important as they pull together to protect themselves and/or their public image. As a result, providing performance data that allow comparisons with other groups is a very powerful tool for increasing group cohesiveness.

Some assignments are clearly better than others at providing such comparisons. In general, the more assignments provide unambiguous performance feedback (especially if it is in a form that enables direct comparisons with similar groups) the better they are at promoting team development. Further, the more immediate the feedback, the greater its value to both learning and group cohesiveness. By contrast, assignments are likely to limit the development of group cohesiveness (and encourage social loafing) if they force groups to do the majority of their work in the absence of feedback. When groups have no way of knowing how they are doing (e.g. when groups are asked to produce some sort of a complex "product" such as a group paper), members are likely to experience a great deal of stress in working with each other. For example, differences in members' work styles often produce a great deal of tension in the group. Members who have a strong preference for a systematic and orderly approach and have time to work on the project often become so anxious that they alienate their peers who either have different time pressures or who feel they do better work when they are faced with a performance deadline.

Rewarding group success. Although it would be wonderful if students or workshop participants would complete group assignments because of a love of learning, if we fail to create a situation in which doing good work as a group "pays off" in some meaningful way, we are, in effect, asking them to behave irrationally. One obvious way to use group rewards as a means of building group cohesiveness is to include group performance in our grading system. Failing to do so will greatly increase the probability that group cohesiveness will be blocked by the fact that students will correctly see themselves competing with other members of their own group.

Including group performance in the grading system is not, however, the most effective way to use rewards for building groups (and minimize social loafing) for three reasons. First, unless the grading system also promotes individual accountability (e.g., grading individual work that prepares students for group work, using a peer evaluation system, etc.), social loafing can still become a serious problem. Second, groups often contain members with very different needs -- what may be an acceptable grade for one student might be a disaster for another. Third, giving grades isn't even a possibility in workshops and many other educational settings in which we should be using group work.

In our judgment, the reward that offers the greatest potential for both classrooms and workshops is the basic human need for social validation. Everyone wants to feel they can offer something of value to others. Thus, by creating a situation where the output from group work will be scrutinized and challenged by peers from other groups, we are creating an environment that promotes both group cohesiveness and learning.

The best and the worst. Based on our experience, the best activity available for building group cohesiveness and minimizing social loafing is the Readiness Assurance Process which constitutes the first four steps in the learning activity sequence in Team Learning (Michaelsen, Watson & Schraeder, 1985; Michaelsen, 1992; Michaelsen & Black, 1994) and the **worst** activity is group term papers. The Readiness Assurance Process is used at the very beginning of each major instructional unit (i.e., prior to any lectures) to ensure that student master basic course content. It involves four steps: 1) individual students complete a test over a set of pre-assigned readings and turn in their answers, 2) groups then re-take the same test and turn in their consensus answers for immediate scoring (group scores are posted on the board to provide immediate cross-group comparisons), 3) groups are given time re-study their assigned readings to prepare written appeals for any questions they have missed, and 4) the instructor provides input that is specifically focused on remediating student misunderstandings that have come to light in the previous three steps of the process. The power of the Readiness Assurance Process comes from the fact that its activities, in combination, clearly meet all four of the criteria for building groups.

By contrast, group term papers seldom provide any support for building group cohesiveness and almost universally result in at least the perception of social loafing. Because writing is inherently an individual activity, the rational way to accomplish the overall task is to divide up the work so that each member independently completes part of the assignment (usually the part that he or she already knows the most about). As a result, there is seldom any significant discussion after the initial division of labor, and feedback is generally unavailable until it is too late to create either individual accountability or meaningful comparisons with other groups. Further, under these conditions, having part of the grade based on group performance is as much of a negative as a positive. Members are well aware that the failure of any member of the group could force the rest to accept a low grade or engage in a last-minute attempt to salvage a disaster. In fact, high-achieving students often express the feeling that getting an acceptable grade on a group term paper feels like having crossed a freeway during rush hour without being run over.

Differences in group process that result from the specific requirements of learning tasks not only affect group cohesiveness; they also have a profound impact on learning. Before we try to link group processes and learning, however, we will briefly set the stage by reviewing some of what is known about "ways" in which we learn, i.e., process information. As a result, the following paragraphs focus on cognitive processes that come into play as we take-in, store, and use ideas and information.

Learning Processes: Implications for Assignment Design

On the surface, what we know would seem to be the sum total of the information to which we have been exposed. Taking in information is, however, only part of the learning process. Information that is taken in and stored in short-term memory decays very rapidly. Thus, from a practical standpoint, what we "know" is more a function of our ability to retrieve and use the information than the sum total of the information that we have taken in.

Impact of what we know. Our ability to learn is profoundly affected by both information to which we have previously been exposed and the way this information is stored in our long-term memory. Most importantly, our capability to learn depends on the extent to which the related components of our memory are clustered into well organized structures. These information structures are important because they provide "hooks" that help establish links between new information that is related to what we already "know" and between the individual components of our existing structures. In addition, the structures provide a backdrop that helps us to recognize what we don't know (i.e., information that doesn't "fit").

Information structures and learning. What we "know," then, is largely a function of the number, complexity and inter-connectedness of the information structures in our long-term memory and, for practical purposes, consists of the information that we are able to retrieve and use. Significant learning has taken place when we increase the amount of information we are able to retrieve and use. This usually occurs when new information motivates us to: 1) add to existing structures, 2) establish new structures, or 3) establish new links within or between existing structures.

Elaborative Rehearsal. If a learning activity exposes us to new information that neatly connects to a "hook" in one of our information structures, then it is simply "attached" to the appropriate link. If new information appears to conflict with existing grouping, the learning process takes a very different, but even more beneficial, course. Initially, we will "search through" our long-term memory to review the linkages upon which the apparent conflict is based. If this review confirms the existence of a conflict, we will be in a state of discomfort until we find a harmonious accommodation. If none is found and the information's credibility is sustained, we are motivated to eliminate the conflict by modifying and/or adding to existing information grouping. This memory retrieval and examination process, called elaborative rehearsal (Craik & Lockhart, 1986), facilitates learning because each stage has a positive impact on our long-term memory. As a result, the greater the extent to which an assignment exposes students or workshop participants to credible information that conflicts with their existing information structures, the greater its impact on their long-term memory.

Promoting the development of higher-level cognitive skills. The importance of providing opportunities for elaborative rehearsal is dramatically illustrated by a series of studies involving learning groups that are summarized in Slavin (1995). In all of the studies, students were divided into four member "Jigsaw" groups. Each member was assigned to become a subject-matter expert with respect to one of four areas and then given the opportunity to teach the material to the other members of his or her Jigsaw team. In most instances, students in Jigsaw groups scored higher on an overall summative test than students from a control group who had been taught with a more traditional method. The positive benefits of the Jigsaw activity, however, were primarily due to students' mastery of the material that they had "taught" to their peers. Hearing someone else explain a set of concepts (i.e., listening to a lecture) had a minimal positive effect as compared to the impact of having to synthesize the information, organize a presentation and present the information to a group of peers.

In two other studies, Lazarowitz (1991) and Lazarowitz and Karsenty (1990) added an additional learning task for the Jigsaw groups. After the Jigsaw peer instruction, each of the groups was given a discovery-oriented problem to solve that required actively using information presented by each of the four subject-matter experts. The most significant finding from these studies was that requiring students to engage in a higher level thinking (Gagne, 1970) increased students' ability to recall and use the information that was originally presented by the other subject-matter experts.

Based on the overall results of the Jigsaw studies, it appears that listening to another peer in a learning group, even when combined with the opportunity to ask clarifying questions, produces only modest gains in long-term memory. On the other hand, learning activities that require higher-level thinking skills (Gagne, 1970) such as acting in a teaching role or using concepts to solve a discovery-oriented problem, produce substantially greater long-term gains in students' ability to recall and use course concepts. Other types of learning activities that focus on using higher level thinking skills have also been shown to produce similar gains compared to simple cognitive tasks such as listening to lectures or going over one's notes. These include taking tests, writing "minute papers", and being exposed to opposing views on a subject then having to resolve the conflicts in the process of making a decision. In combination, these findings convincingly argue that he long-term impact of group work will be much greater if group assignments go beyond simply exposing learners to new information by requiring them to actively engage in the use of higher-level cognitive skills.

Phrasing Assignments to Promote the Use of Higher-level Cognitive Skills.

The degree to which assignments stimulate higher-level cognitive skills (i.e., elaborative rehearsal) is largely a function of what we ask students to "produce." For example, suppose an English composition instructor wanted to ensure that his or her students were able to recognize the effective use of active vs. passive voice in written communication.

stimulate higher-level thinking because students could "make-a-list" by simply extracting items from one or more reference sources and recording them in another location. Assignment #2 is considerably better. Having to "make-a-choice" would require students to examine critically the sentences in the sample passage and use the criteria that define active vs. passive voice to identify examples of active and passive voice. Alternative #3 would provide the most practice using higher-level cognitive skills for two reasons. First, students could not complete task #3 unless they could also complete tasks #1 and #2. Second, as is typical of "make-a-specific-choice" assignments, picking a single best example of correct use of passive voice would require students to use/develop a number of higher-level cognitive skills. At a minimum, these would include making multiple comparisons and discriminations, analysis of content information and, verification of rule application.

Implications for Effective Group Assignments

Although "make-a-specific-choice" assignments are beneficial for individual students working alone, they produce the greatest gains in conjunction with learning groups. In part, this occurs because students/workshop participants have an additional source of motivation to take the assignment seriously. In addition, group interaction provides two additional opportunities to stimulate active learning. One is during discussions within the groups. The other occurs during subsequent class discussions (i.e., between groups). Further, when used in a group context, "Make-a-specific-choice" assignments increase learning in each step of the process and set the stage for greater learning.

Individual preparation for group work. As long as group members are given the assignment as preparation for group work, having students make a specific choice ensures that members will be individually far more accountable for having engaged in higher-level thinking than is the case with "make-a-list" assignments for three reasons. First, learners have to use higher-level thinking skills in order to make choices. Second, members expect to be asked to share their choice with their group. Third, they are also aware that, unless the group is in complete agreement, the differences will be so evident that proponents of each of the alternatives will almost certainly be asked to explain the reasons behind their choices. As a result, "make-a-specific-choice" assignments motivate most students/workshop participants to enter the group discussion with a with a clearly defined position and the ability to defend it.

Discussions within groups. The difference between "make-a-list" and "make-a-specific-choice" assignments is even more evident in intra-team discussion. Listing possibilities tends to be a low energy team task for several reasons. One is that a search for what should be on a list focuses on quantity rather than quality. Another is that once several items go on the list, it is easy for quieter and/or less self-assured participants to get "off the hook" by saying that their ideas are already listed. Finally, making a list seldom leads to a feeling of pride in the group output because the majority of the items are likely to be in common with other groups.

By contrast, when groups are asked to select a single best choice based on specific criteria and know that other groups have been given the same assignment, members are likely to engage in an intense give-and-take discussion of why any given choice is better than another. No one wants to be the only group to have made a particular choice and not be able to present a clear and cogent rationale for their position. As a result, most groups will engage in "make-a-specific-choice" tasks with a great deal of energy and are also likely to be willing and able to defend their choices.

Discussions between groups. Group assignments phrased in "make-a-specific-choice" terms produce their greatest gains in subsequent class discussions (i.e., between-groups). Two of the benefits come from the simplicity of the output. One is that they invariably promote group accountability because any differences between groups are absolutely clear. For example, an assignment that asked groups to select the single best example of an appropriate use of passive voice would produce a much more productive class discussion than an assignment that asked groups to identify examples of appropriate use of active and passive voice. Comparing "best examples" is likely to produce a more intense and informative discussion than either listing examples or the choice of a clear example. When comparing "best examples," groups have a vested interest in defending their position and the discussion will focus on the reasons that one choice is better than another.

By contrast, group assignments that result in either lists or non-specific choices often result in low-energy class discussion and allow relatively poor group analyses to go unchallenged. The lack of energy results from the fact that groups tend to be far more interested in their own work than that of other groups. Poor analysis often goes unchallenged because: 1) having students/workshop participants either make a list or a non-specific choice is likely to produce so much data that the task of finding something to challenge can be quite difficult and 2) the absence of clear comparisons allows groups to overlook inconsistencies in both their own and other groups' analyses.

Group cohesiveness. Another important benefit of properly designed "make-a-specific-choice" group assignments is their positive impact on cohesiveness. Because reaching consensus on a difficult choice requires a great deal of thought and effort, students/workshop participants intuitively realize that differences between teams represent an important source of feedback. Thus, because differences between team choices are so clear, they represent a significant external threat. By contrast, "make-a-list" assignments seldom promote group cohesiveness because the output is poorly suited for inter-group comparisons. This becomes most apparent when groups share the results of their discussions. Even though groups generally do a pretty good job of making lists, there is almost always a "nose-dive" in the energy level when the groups "report" to the class. In fact, simply getting students/workshop participants to pay attention to each other as representatives go over each item in their list can be a serious problem. Differences that groups might otherwise take pride in and be motivated to defend, are both obscured and diminished in significance by the sheer volume of data.

Assignments that Facilitate Inter-group Comparisons.

There are two keys to ensuring that "make-a-specific choice" assignments facilitate inter-group comparisons. One is keeping the "output" as simple as possible. The other is organizing the inter-group sharing process to minimize the amount of time used in a lecture-like mode (i.e., a series of representatives giving a report of what happened in their group).

For example, suppose a marketing instructor wanted to create a "make-a-specific choice" assignment that would ensure him or her that students understood the key variables that should be considered in selecting a site upon which to locate a new business. One way to word the assignment would be, "Select what you think would be the ideal site to locate a new dry cleaning establishment in ... (i.e., filling in the name of a specific city about which students could gain access to relevant data), identify, and be prepared to explain the rationale for the single most important site selection factor that led to your decision."

Although the assignment involves making a specific choice, the degree to which it would support inter-group comparisons depends on both the specific "product" that was used to represent their choice and the nature of the group reporting process. One common approach would be to assign each of four groups to make a 10-minute presentation revealing their chosen location and the rationale for selecting it followed by a few minutes for questions and class discussion.

Alternatively, the instructor could require students to come to class having made their choice and, instead of using class time for presentations, he or she could:

1) Give each group a post-it-note with their group number on it, a felt-tipped marker and a legal-sized sheet of paper.

2) Allow 5-minutes to decide on and record their single most important reason for their decision.

3) Require groups (after 5 minutes), to place their post-it on their selected location on a city map attached to the classroom wall.

4) Allow groups 10 minutes to formulate questions they would like to ask the other groups.

5) Use the remainder of the class for questions and discussion.

In this example, the "post-it-note" version of the assignment would provide far more explicit intergroup comparisons. With presentations, the differences are obscured by three factors. First, the sheer volume of data in three other 10-minute presentations makes it difficult for students to keep track. Second, the relevant facts are presented over a 40-minute span. As a result, the key points will be temporally separated by far less significant information. Third, since the groups are likely to use a variety of presentation modes, establishing links between key ideas is likely to seem like comparing apples and oranges. By contrast, using the "post-it-note" approach ensures that, instead of being overwhelmed with data, students are exposed to a simultaneous, common, permanent, and highly visual representation of only the essential data: 1) the proposed locations and 2) the foundation of each group's rationale for their choice. Further, they have a designated time to carefully process and digest the information in an integrated way.

A Checklist for Effective Group Activities.

Probably the most important key in designing effective group assignments is viewing the entire context within which they will be used. This includes taking into account the developmental level of the groups, individual preparation for group work, discussions within groups, post-group class discussions, and the extent to which the group will work together again. The following checklist provides prompts for taking these factors into account as you evaluate and or design group assignments.

Making Good Group Assignments into Great Ones

Regardless of its primary intent, every learning activity affects learning in two very different ways. First, the specific characteristics of the activity determine how much active learning can be achieved by its use. Second, each activity inherently fosters (or inhibits) the peer interactions that have a major impact on team development.. Further, modifying an activity in an attempt to change the impact on either dimension is likely to affect the other.

For example, we have an agronomist colleague who wants his students to develop the ability to recognize the weeds that commonly infest turf grass lawns in our region. Initially, he used an assignment that required groups to "identify and appropriately tag an example of each weed variety growing in plot #1 [which he had laid out] on the lawn on the east side of this building". The assignment worked quite well but, he decided to modify the group portion of the activity in an attempt to increase its value for building cohesiveness. The revised assignment uses 5 plots (one for each group in the class) and requires an additional 20 minutes to complete. During the first 10 minutes the group members, working individually within their team's plot, find and temporarily tag an example of each weed variety. During the next 20 minutes, the groups: agree on (and permanently tag) a sample of each weed variety in their plot (and receive 10 points for each correctly tagged weed variety) and, 2) prepare for a "weed finders challenge" (WFC). During the WFC, groups have 5 minutes to examine each others' plots and "challenge" incorrectly tagged weeds. If their challenge is valid, they receive 10 bonus points but, if the challenge is bogus, they lose 10 points to the group who elicited the challenge.

Although the changes were modest in nature, they produced positive changes in all four of the factors that affect group cohesiveness. The assignment now provides rewards for group work (the opportunity to earn points for correctly tagging weeds and extra points by successfully challenging other groups). The assignment provides external comparison/feedback (by giving other groups the opportunity to challenge each other). The assignment produces high levels of group interaction (reaching consensus on your own samples and preparing members to scout other plots). Finally, the assignment promotes individual accountability on both ends (individual tagging prior to group work and individuals serving as scouts during the WFC). As a result, the assignment is much more effective in building group cohesiveness. Groups typically use the first half of their time to make sure they have a correctly tagged sample of each weed variety. Then they turn their attention to preparing for the WFC by:

1) preparing members to scout for a potential challenge because they don't have time to go to each of the other plots as a group and 2) shifting their tags to atypical examples of the weed varieties in an attempt to "set-up" other groups for a bogus challenge.

Even though the impact on cohesiveness has been highly positive, the impact on learning has been even greater. The knowledge that they will have to work on their own causes group members to be more serious about advance preparation. Thus, members start out with a reasonably high level of understanding that is further enhanced during the group discussions in preparation for the weed finders' challenge. Nor does the learning end there. Many of the students who have participated in the weed finders challenge report that they can't have a picnic any more without thinking about what kind of weeds are going to be covered by their picnic blanket.

Energy -- the Acid Test for Effective Group Activities

Our colleague's experience with modifying the group assignment for his agronomy class illustrates two key concepts about effective group assignments. First, the best way to increase the effectiveness of group assignments is to focus on increasing the extent to which they build group cohesiveness. Assignments simply will not increase group cohesiveness unless they produce a great deal of task-focused energy. Thus, if you ask yourself the question, "How can I change this assignment so that it will increase group cohesiveness?" you are also asking, "How can I change this assignment so that students/workshop participants will commit a higher level of energy to this learning task?" Second, the single best indicator of the effectiveness of a group assignment is what happens when groups share the results of their discussions with the class as a whole. The higher the energy (i.e., the extent to which groups are interested in and willing to spontaneously challenge each others thinking and defend their own), the more confident you can be that: 1) they have taken their group work seriously and 2) their ability to tackle even more difficult learning tasks has been significantly enhanced.

Overall, we hope that four messages have come through in this paper. First, group activities and assignments can be a highly effective tool for developing both students' mastery of basic conceptual material and their higher-level thinking and problem solving skills. Second, the vast majority of student or workshop participants dysfunctional behaviors (e.g., social loafing, one or two members dominating the discussion, etc.) and complaints (e.g., having to carry the dead wood, the instructor isn't teaching, etc.) are the result of bad assignments not bad learners. Third, the key to designing effective group assignments is to maximize the extent to which the learning tasks promote the development of cohesive learning groups. Finally, the single best way to gauge the effectiveness of group assignments is the observe the level of energy that is present when the results of the small group discussions are reported to the class as a whole.

Outdoor Action Guide to Group Dynamics & Leadership by Rick Curtis

Group Development

An Effective Group

- Has a clear understanding of its goals: overall and immediate.
- Is flexible in selecting its procedure as it works toward its goals.
- Has achieved a high degree of communication and understanding among its members. Communication of personal feelings and attitudes as well as ideas occurs in direct and open fashion because it is considered important to the work of the group.
- Is able to initiate and carry out an effective decision-making, carefully considering minority viewpoints

and securing the commitment of all members to important decisions.

- Achieves an appropriate balance between group productivity and the satisfaction of individual needs.
- Provides for sharing of leadership responsibilities.
- Has a high degree of cohesiveness (attractiveness to its members).
- Makes intelligent use of the differing abilities if its members.
- Can be objective about reviewing its own processes. Can face problems and adjust to needed modification.
- Maintains a balance between emotional and rational behavior, channeling emotionally into productive group effort.

Achieving a Cooperative Group Structure

1. Members must interact, give and receive help from one another, and share ideas, information, and resources to help accomplish the group's goals.
2. The group goal of getting the task done at the highest level possible must be accepted by everyone, and members need to develop commitment to the group goal.
3. Because the possibility exists of different group members doing different sub-tasks, groups may divide the labor in various ways to accomplish their goals.
4. Rewards, if any, must be based upon the quality and quantity of group performance, not individual performance.

Basic Stages of Group Development

There are several basic stages that new groups go through as they move to becoming effective as a group. These stages parallel the Situational Leadership Model and as shown, different styles of leadership tend to work best at different points in the overall development of the group.

1. **Forming (Getting Acquainted)** - This first stage is characterized by a sense of uncertainty and awkwardness and perhaps anxiety. Participants may be unsure of what to do and how to do it. The "rules of the road"-group norms and standards have yet to be defined and participants are eagerly looking to find out what is okay and not okay. This phase often shows as tentativeness or even some anxiety on the part of the participants. Leaders need to set the tone for group behavior, activities, and interactions (see Establishing Group Norms below). Most people are polite as they try to put their "best foot forward." The result is a superficial level of harmony and cooperation. This serves the purpose of getting the group started and off the ground in terms of motivation and commitment. Members may tend to verbalize how close they feel to each other, and may develop quite a group spirit due to successful task accomplishment. Leadership at this point should be a combination of High Task/Low Relationship (Telling) in terms of teaching skills and establishing norms moving to High Task/High Relationship (Selling) to get everyone involved and interacting in the group.
2. **Storming (Struggling Forward)** - This next stage is characterized by individual assertive behavior which may result in some group instability. Participants have begun to feel comfortable enough with their new environment to take some risks in revealing more of their personalities. Each person wants to feel a sense of individual importance and influence on the group - "finding a niche." This becomes more evident as increasing responsibility is shifted to the group as they move into moderate levels of maturity. The Leadership style which may be most effective are High Task/High Relationship (Selling). Leaders should not be surprised if some conflicts

develop in the group at this stage. This is part of the natural process of the group becoming self-sustaining.

3. **Norming (Becoming Personal)** - This stage is characterized by a growth of affection and establishment of personal relationships. Participants will begin to take responsibility for resolving conflicts and strengthening friendships. The Leadership style which may be most effective is Low Task/High Relationship (Participating) since the group is competent regarding tasks but needs assistance and support in terms of relationships.
4. **Performing (Working Together)** - This stage is characterized by harmony among group members. Participants look outwards to see how other people in the group are doing to make sure all are supported. Decision making and problem solving will be shared within the group. At this stage the group is mature enough to attend to its own needs both in terms of task and relationship matters. The leadership style which would be most effective would be Low Task/Low Relationship (Delegating).
5. **Transference** - This final part of the group process is essential in making sure that the trip is not remembered as "just a fun couple days in the woods." It is important that participants be able to transfer the things which they have learned about themselves and being in a group back to their regular lives. This is accomplished through the debriefing process discussed in below in Transferring the Experience.

Establishing Group Norms

Establishing norms is an important part of the first stage of group development, letting people learn "the rules of the road." Many of the group norms that we use in OA are actually underlying goals for the experience (like group cooperation, minimal impact, etc.). Group norms can be established in three ways:

- **Stating** - telling/explaining to people how to behave, e.g. this is how to wear a pack.
- **Modeling** - demonstrating behavior for others to adopt, e.g. leaders picking up trash along the trail.
- **Importing** - bringing in behavior customary in other social situations, e.g. people will going off into the woods for privacy to go to the bathroom.

These methods often must be combined in order to work effectively. For example, if you want to reinforce minimal impact camping practices you will need to state it as a goal, explain how to accomplish it, and model the behavior. If the leader simply tells people to pick up trash along the trail, but then walks right by trash without picking it up, the participants become confused as to the norm and may assume that the instruction was merely lip service. Remember, at the beginning of a trip, participants may not know what to expect and may not have previous experience in the outdoors. Direct demonstration is the best way to get things across in this early stage. Before the trip goes out, think about what sorts of group norms you want to convey to the group before leaving campus as well as what things you will need to cover during the trip. Below are some examples of things to present to the group.

Norms to Present Pre-Trip

- Group Cooperation (everyone needs to do their share)
- Minimal Impact Camping (idea not specific techniques)
- Safety
- Substance Free trip

Norms to Present During the Trip

- Challenge by Choice
- Good Communication and Listening between group members
- Debriefing

- Respect for Others

Group Decision Making

During the course of a trip, there are a number of decisions that will need to be made by the whole group. These might include things like where to camp, which route to take, whether to rest for the afternoon or do a side hike, etc. Group decision making can be a powerful learning and growth tool for the group. It can also be a place for conflict to develop. The first thing to determine is whether it is a decision that can and should be made by the group, or with input from the group, or is it a decision to be made solely by the leaders. Obviously some issue, such as those that involve safety, will be made by the leaders. To present such a decision to the group suggests that they have authority to make the decision, and if the leaders disagree, they must countermand the group's decision. Also some decision-making can lead to splintering the group. Both of these can lead to bad feelings by the group members and damage the positive group spirit and interaction leaders have worked to facilitate. Avoid this problem by thinking ahead and determining what decisions are appropriate for the group to make. It may be better for the leaders to make the decision from their status as authorities, that to give the decision to the group and have the process lead to negative outcomes. Leaders will also need to decide if they should be involved in the decision process, or "sit it out." Sometime the presence and perceived authority of the leaders can slant the decision making process. However, in certain situations, this can work to your advantage as a leader. Making good group decisions involves a process, which the leaders may have to state or model as a norm for the group to follow.

Decision Strategies

- **Authority Decides** - In this case the decision is made by the leaders by virtue of their role of being responsible for the trip or by some person determined to have the greatest knowledge about the topic. This process can be very effective when the individual(s) have significantly more knowledge than the other members of the group. It is also very efficient in terms of time. In some cases, getting feedback from the group may be essential for the leaders to have all the facts in order to make a good decision. For example, if the leaders have to decide about changing the route, they need to know the physical and mental state of all the participants. The most common scenario for this decision making process is a safety or emergency situation. Here the leaders need to take charge of the group. Keep in mind that some individuals, even though they may be the most knowledgeable, may not be good at making decisions. Making effective decisions is a skill that all leaders should develop. If things seem to be breaking down and a decision is not being made, you may have to move to another method.

- **Majority Vote** - In this case members of the group are polled and the option that receives support from the greatest number in the group is chosen. This strategy works well if everyone agrees to be bound by it, and if everyone feels they have a chance to express their viewpoints and needs. However, it can lead to splitting of the group. Once again leaders should evaluate if this method will be a positive or negative experience for the group.
- **Consensus** - This is the most effective method of making a group decision in terms of members feeling included. Consensus decision making means reaching a decision that all members of the group are willing to support at some level. In order to reach this point, everyone in the group must be given ample time to express their view and time to express their disagreement with other's views. Through a process of negotiation, the group moves to an idea that everyone can place some level of support in. this process can take a great deal of

time and "perfect consensus" is almost never reached. Make sure that you have the time before embarked on this as you approach. It is counter-productive to start with the consensus process and then have to give it up to make the decision some other way because you don't have enough time.

In all of these strategies it is important for leaders to model good listening and communication skills. Leaders may need to act as facilitators for effective communication through such things as asking people not to interrupt others, quieting dominant members of the group, and asking quieter members to speak up.

Group Decision Making Process

1. Set goal(s) & prioritize them
2. Brainstorm options for achieving goals
3. Evaluate the different options and examine how the options meet the goal(s)
4. Determine the decision-making strategy to be used (see above)
5. Decide on an option using one of the following criteria
    - Best serves highest priority goals
    - Best serves all goals
    - Serves goals without creating any negative outcomes
    - Creates the least negative outcomes

Chapter 3

Role of Education in Cultural Reform

The word culture, from the Latin root colere (to inhabit, to cultivate, or to honor), generally refers to patterns of human activity and the symbolic structures that give such activity significance. Different definitions of "culture" reflect different theoretical orientations for understanding, or criteria for valuing, human activity. Anthropologists most commonly use the term "culture" to refer to the universal human capacity to classify, codify and communicate their experiences symbolically. This capacity is a defining feature of the genus Homo.

Defining culture

Different definitions of culture reflect different theories for understanding - or criteria for valuing - human activity.

Sir Edward B. Tylor wrote in 1871 that "culture or civilization, taken in its wide ethnographic sense, is that complex whole which includes knowledge, belief, art, morals, law, custom, and any other capabilities and habits acquired by man as a member of society", while a 2002 document from the United Nations agency UNESCO states that culture is the "set of distinctive spiritual, material, intellectual and emotional features of society or a social group, and that it encompasses, in addition to art and literature, lifestyles, ways of living together, value systems, traditions and beliefs". [UNESCO, 2002] While these two definitions range widely, they do not exhaust the many uses of this concept - in 1952 Alfred Kroeber and Clyde Kluckhohn compiled a list of more than 200 different definitions of culture in their book, Culture: A Critical Review of Concepts and Definitions.

Culture as civilization

Many people today use a conception of "culture" that developed in Europe during the 18th and early 19th centuries. This idea of culture then reflected inequalities within European societies, and between European powers and their colonies around the world. It identifies "culture" with "civilization" and contrasts the combined concept with "nature". According to this thinking, one can classify some countries as more civilized than others, and some people as more cultured than others. Thus some cultural theorists have actually tried to eliminate popular or mass culture from the definition of culture. Theorists like Matthew Arnold (1822-1888) or the Leavises regard culture as simply the result of "the best that has been thought and said in the world" (Arnold, 1960: 6), thus labeling anything that doesn't fit into this category as chaos or anarchy. On this account, culture links closely with social cultivation: the progressive refinement of human behavior. Arnold consistently uses the word this way: "... culture being a pursuit of our total perfection by means of getting to know, on all the matters which most concern us, the best which has been thought and said in the world".

In practice, culture referred to élite goods and activities such as haute cuisine, high fashion or haute couture, museum-caliber art and classical music, and the word cultured described people who knew about, and took part in, these activities. For example, someone who used 'culture' in the sense of 'cultivation' might argue that classical music "is" more refined than music produced by working-class people such as punk rock or than the indigenous music traditions of aboriginal peoples of Australia.

People who use "culture" in this way tend not to use it in the plural as "cultures". They do not believe that distinct cultures exist, each with their own internal logic and values; but rather that only a single standard of refinement suffices, against which one can measure all groups. Thus, according to this worldview, people with different customs from those who regard themselves as cultured do not usually count as "having a different culture"; but class as "uncultured". People lacking "culture" often seemed more "natural," and observers often defended (or criticized) elements of high culture for repressing "human nature".

From the 18th century onwards, some social critics have accepted this contrast between cultured and uncultured, but have stressed the interpretation of refinement and of sophistication as corrupting and unnatural developments which obscure and distort people's essential nature. On this account, folk music (as produced by working-class people) honestly expresses a natural way of life, and classical music seems superficial and decadent. Equally, this view often portrays non-Western people as 'noble savages' living authentic unblemished lives, uncomplicated and uncorrupted by the highly-stratified capitalist systems of the West.

Today most social scientists reject the monadic conception of culture, and the opposition of culture to nature. They recognize non-élites as just as cultured as élites (and non-Westerners as just as civilized) - simply regarding them as just cultured in a different way. Thus social observers contrast the "high" culture of élites to "popular" or pop culture, meaning goods and activities produced for, and consumed by, non-élite people or the masses. (Note that some classifications relegate both high and low cultures to the status of subcultures.)

Culture as worldview

During the Romantic era, scholars in Germany, especially those concerned with nationalist movements -- such as the nationalist struggle to create a "Germany" out of diverse principalities, and the nationalist struggles by ethnic minorities against the Austro-Hungarian Empire -- developed a more inclusive notion of culture as "worldview". In this mode of thought, a distinct and incommensurable world view characterizes each ethnic group. Although more inclusive than earlier views, this approach to culture still allowed for distinctions between "civilized" and "primitive" or "tribal" cultures.

By the late 19th century, anthropologists had adopted and adapted the term culture to a broader definition that they could apply to a wider variety of societies. Attentive to the theory of evolution, they assumed that all human beings evolved equally, and that the fact that all humans have cultures must in some way result from human evolution. They also showed some reluctance to use biological evolution to explain differences between specific cultures -- an approach that either exemplified a form of, or legitimized forms of, racism. They believed that biological evolution would produce a most inclusive notion of culture, a concept that anthropologists could apply equally to non-literate and to literate societies, or to nomadic and to sedentary societies. They argued that through the course of their evolution, human beings evolved a universal human capacity to classify experiences, and to encode and communicate them symbolically. Since human individuals learned and taught these symbolic systems, the systems began to develop independently of biological evolution (in other words, one human being can learn a belief, value, or way of doing something from another, even if the two humans do not share a biological relationship). That this capacity for symbolic thinking and social learning stems from human evolution confounds older arguments about nature versus nurture. Thus Clifford Geertz (1973: 33 ff.) has argued that human physiology and neurology developed in conjunction with the first cultural activities, and Middleton concluded that human "'instincts' were culturally formed".

People living apart from one another develop unique cultures, but elements of different cultures can easily spread from one group of people to another. Culture changes dynamically and people can (must?) teach and learn culture, making it a potentially rapid form of adaptation to change in physical conditions. Anthropologists view culture as not only as a product of biological evolution but as a supplement to it, as the main means of human adaptation to the world.

This view of culture as a symbolic system with adaptive functions, and one which varies from place to place, led anthropologists to conceive of different cultures as defined by distinct patterns (or structures) of enduring, arbitrary, conventional sets of meaning, which took concrete form in a variety of artifacts such as myths and rituals, tools, the design of housing, and the planning of villages. Anthropologists thus distinguish between material culture and symbolic culture, not only because each reflects different kinds of human activity, but also because they constitute different kinds of data that require different methodologies.

This view of culture, which came to dominate between World War I and World War II, implied that each culture had bounds and demanded interpretation as a whole, on its own terms. There resulted a belief in cultural relativism; the belief that one had to understand an individual's actions in terms of his or her culture; that one had to understand a specific cultural artifact (a ritual, for example) in terms of the larger symbolic system of which it forms a part.

Nevertheless, the belief that culture comprises symbolical codes and can thus pass via teaching from one person to another meant that cultures, although bounded, would change. Cultural change could result from invention and innovation, but it could also result from contact between two cultures. Under peaceful conditions, contact between two cultures can lead to people "borrowing" (really, learning) from one another (diffusion or transculturation). Under conditions of violence or political inequality, however, people of one society can "steal" cultural artifacts from another, or impose cultural artifacts on another (acculturation). Diffusion of innovations theory presents a research-based model for how, when and why people adopt new ideas.

All human societies have participated in these processes of diffusion, transculturation, and acculturation, and few anthropologists today see cultures as bounded. Modern anthropologists argue that instead of understanding a cultural artifact in terms of its own culture, one needs to understand it in terms of a broader history involving contact and relations with other cultures.

In addition to the aforementioned processes, migration on a major scale has characterized the world, particularly since the days of Columbus. Phenomena such as colonial expansion and forced migration through slavery became prominent.

As a result, many societies have become culturally heterogeneous. Some anthropologists have argued nevertheless that some unifying cultural system bound heterogeneous societies, and that it offers advantages to understand heterogenous elements as subcultures. Others have argued that no unifying or coordinating cultural system exists, and that one must understand heterogeneous elements together as forming a multicultural society. The spread of the doctrine of multiculturalism has coincided with a resurgence of identity politics, which involve demands for the recognition of social subgroups' cultural uniqueness.

Sociobiologists argue that observers can best understand many aspects of culture in the light of the concept of the meme, first introduced by Richard Dawkins in his 1976 book The Selfish Gene. Dawkins suggests the existence of units of culture - memes - roughly analogous to genes in evolutionary biology. Although this view has gained some popular currency, anthropologists generally reject it.

Culture as values, norms, and artifacts

Another common way of understanding culture sees it as consisting of three elements:

- values
- norms
- artifacts.

Values comprise ideas about what in life seems important. They guide the rest of the culture. Norms consist of expectations of how people will behave in different situations. Each culture has different methods, called sanctions, of enforcing its norms. Sanctions vary with the importance of the norm; norms that a society enforces formally have the status of laws. Artifacts — things, or material culture — derive from the culture's values and norms.

Julian Huxley gives a slightly different division, into inter-related "mentifacts", "socifacts" and "artifacts", for ideological, sociological, and technological subsystems respectively. Socialization, in Huxley's view, depends on the belief subsystem. The sociological subsystem governs interaction between people. Material objects and their use make up the technological subsystem.

As a rule, archeologists focus on material culture whereas cultural anthropologists focus on symbolic culture, although ultimately both groups maintain interests in the relationships between these two dimensions. Moreover, anthropologists understand "culture" to refer not only to consumption goods, but to the general processes which produce such goods and give them meaning, and to the social relationships and practices in which such objects and processes become embedded.

Culture as patterns of products and activities

In the early 20th century, anthropologists understood culture to refer not to a set of discrete products or activities (whether material or symbolic) but rather to underlying patterns of products and activities. Moreover, they assumed that such patterns had clear bounds (thus, some people confuse "culture" with the society that has a particular culture).

In the case of smaller societies, in which people merely fell into categories of age, gender, household and descent group, anthropologists believed that people more-or-less shared the same set of values and conventions. In the case of larger societies, in which people undergo further categorization by region, race, ethnicity, and class, anthropologists came to believe that members of the same society often had highly contrasting values and conventions. They thus used the term subculture to identify the cultures of parts of larger societies. Since subcultures reflect the position of a segment of society vis a vis other segments and the society as a whole, they often reveal processes of domination and resistance.

The 20th century also saw the popularization of the idea of corporate culture - distinct and malleable within the context of an employing organization or of a workplace.

Culture as Symbols

The symbolic view of culture, the legacy of Clifford Geertz (1973) and Victor Turner (1967), holds symbols to be both the practices of social actors and the context that gives such practices meaning. Anthony P. Cohen (1985) writes of the "symbolic gloss" which allows social actors to use common symbols to communicate and understand each other while still imbuing these symbols with personal significance and meanings. Symbols provide the limits of cultured thought. Members of a culture rely on these symbols to frame their thoughts and expressions in intelligible terms. In short, symbols make culture possible, reproducible and readable. They are the "webs of significance" in Weber's sense that, to quote Pierre Bourdieu (1977), "give regularity, unity and systematicity to the practices of a group...".

Culture as stabilizing mechanism

Modern cultural theory also considers the possibility that (a) culture itself is a product of stabilization tendencies inherent in evolutionary pressures toward self-similarity and self-cognition of societies as wholes, or tribalisms. See Steven Wolfram "A new kind of science" on iterated simple algorithms from genetic unfolding, from which the concept of culture as an operating mechanism can be developed, and Richard Dawkins "The extended phenotype" for discussion of genetic and memetic stability over time, through negative feedback mechanisms, such as Wikipedia.

Cultural change

Cultures, by predisposition, both embrace and resist change dependence of culture traits. For example, men and women have complementary roles in many cultures. One sex might desire changes that affect the other, as happened in the second half of the 20th century in western cultures.

Cultural change can come about due to the environment, to inventions (and other internal influences), and to contact with other cultures. For example, the end of the last ice age helped lead to the invention of agriculture, which in its turn brought about many cultural innovations.

In diffusion, the form of something moves from one culture to another, but not its meaning. For example, hamburgers, mundane in the United States, seemed exotic when introduced into China. "Stimulus diffusion" refers to an element of one culture leading to an invention in another. Diffusions of innovations theory presents a research-based model for why and when individuals and cultures adopt new ideas, practices, and products.

"Acculturation" has different meanings, but in this context refers to replacement of the traits of one culture with those of another, such as happened to certain Native American tribes and to many indigenous peoples across the globe during the process of colonization

Related processes on an individual level include assimilation (adoption of a different culture by an individual) and transculturation.

Propagating culture

Insofar as culture grows and changes naturally within human society, it requires little or no formal propagation. Families or age-based peer-groups will instinctively foster (and develop) their own cultural norms.

But few cultures act in such a laissez faire manner. Most societies develop some sort of religion or similar basis for inculcating and preserving established or "correct" cultural behavior. And many societies take the task of education out of the hands of priests and shamans and place it on a wider footing, so that the young (at least) gain a practical and emotional identification with a standardised version of their nurturing culture.

Groups of immigrants, exiles, or minorities often form cultural associations or clubs to preserve their own cultural roots in the face of a surrounding (generally more locally-dominant) culture. Thus the world has acquired many Garibaldi Clubs, Pushkin Societies, and underground schools.

On a broader scale, many countries market their cultural heritage internationally. This occurs not only in the promotion of tourism (importing money), but also in cultural development abroad (exporting ideas). Note the roles of cultural attachés in embassies and the function of specific organizations devoted to propagating the mother-culture, its language and its ideologies abroad, for example the work of:

- the Alliance française
- the British Council
- the Fulbright Program
- the Goethe-Institut
- the Instituto Cervantes

Cultural studies

Cultural studies developed in the late 20th century, in part through the re-introduction of Marxist thought into sociology, and in part through the articulation of sociology and other academic disciplines such as literary criticism. This movement aimed to focus on the analysis of subcultures in capitalist societies. Following the non-anthropological tradition, cultural studies generally focus on the study of consumption goods (such as fashion, art, and literature). Because the 18th- and 19th-century distinction between "high" and "low" culture seems inappropriate to apply to the mass-produced and mass-marketed consumption goods which cultural studies analyses, these scholars refer instead to "popular culture".

Today, some anthropologists have joined the project of cultural studies. Most, however, reject the identification of culture with consumption goods. Furthermore, many now reject the notion of culture as bounded, and consequently reject the notion of subculture. Instead, they see culture as a complex web of shifting patterns that link people in different locales and that link social formations of different scales. According to this view, any group can construct its own cultural identity.

Role of Education in Cultural Changes

Multicultural education means different things to different people. However, the differences are not as great, confusing, or contradictory as some critics and analysts claim. Many of these differences are more semantic than substantive, a reflection of the developmental level in the field and the disciplinary orientation of advocates. One should expect people who have been involved in a discipline or educational movement for a long time to understand and talk about it differently from those who are new to it. Similarly, educators who look at schooling from the vantage point of sociology, psychology, or economics will have differing views of the key concerns of schooling. Yet, these disparate analysts may agree on which issues are the most critical ones. Such differences over means coupled with widespread agreement on substance are naturally found in discussions of multicultural education. But this diversity should not be a problem, especially when we consider that multicultural education is all about plurality.

The field includes educational scholars, researchers, and practitioners from a wide variety of personal, professional, philosophical, political, and pedagogical backgrounds. Therefore, we should expect that they will use different points of reference in discussing ethnic diversity and cultural pluralism. Yet, when allowances are made for these differences, a consensus on the substantive components of multicultural education quickly emerges. Such agreement is evident in areas such as the key content dimensions, value priorities, the justification for multicultural education, and its expected outcomes. Only when these fundamentals are articulated do variations emerge.

Some advocates talk about expected outcomes, while others consider the major determining factor to be the group being studied; the arena of school action is the primary focus for one set of advocates, and still others are most concerned with distinctions between theory and practice. Some people are selective about where to begin and what to emphasize in cultural pluralism. Others are more inclusive and want its impact to be felt in all dimensions and on every level. Regardless of these variations, all conceptions of multicultural education share four characteristics: (1) they are based upon a common set of assumptions, (2) they evolve out of common concerns, (3) they contain common guidelines for action, (4) they share a desire to make cultural pluralism and ethnic diversity integral parts of the educational process.

When planning for multicultural education in school programs, it is important to allow different conceptions of multicultural education to be expressed in the school decisionmaking process rather than to insist on one definition. Conceptions of multicultural education contain value beliefs and reflect the varying levels of understanding among people involved in the school decisionmaking process. Conceptions of multicultural education and the value beliefs within them delineate the scope, focus, and boundaries of the field of multicultural education. These conceptions are guidelines for action and need to be clearly understood early in the process of making educational decisions. Accordingly, this synthesis includes various conceptions and definitions of multicultural education and outlines the implications of these definitions for practice.

Definitions of Multicultural Education

Definitions of multicultural education vary. Some definitions rely on the cultural characteristics of diverse groups, while others emphasize social problems (particularly those associated with oppression), political power, and the reallocation of economic resources. Some restrict their focus to people of color, while others include all major groups that are different in any way from mainstream Americans. Other definitions limit multicultural education to characteristics of local schools, and still others provide directions for school reform in all settings regardless of their characteristics. The goals of these diverse types of multicultural education range from bringing more information about various groups to textbooks, to combatting racism, to restructuring the entire school enterprise and reforming society to make schools more culturally fair, accepting, and balanced. For this reason, the field of multicultural education is referred to interchangeably as multicultural education, education that is multicultural, and antiracist education.

The following are the most frequently used definitions of multicultural education:

- An idea, an educational reform movement, and a process intended to change the structure of educational institutions so that all students have an equal chance to achieve academic success
- A philosophy that stresses the importance, legitimacy, and vitality of ethnic and cultural diversity in shaping the lives of individuals, groups, and nations
- A reform movement that changes all components of the educational enterprise, including its underlying values, procedural rules, curricula, instructional materials, organizational structure, and governance policies to reflect cultural pluralism

- An ongoing process that requires long term investments of time and effort as well as carefully planned and monitored actions (Banks & Banks, 1993).
- Institutionalizing a philosophy of cultural pluralism within the educational system that is grounded in principles of equality, mutual respect, acceptance and understanding, and moral commitment to social justice (Baptiste, 1979)
- Structuring educational priorities, commitments, and processes to reflect the cultural pluralism of the United States and to ensure the survival of group heritages that make up society, following American democratic ideals (AACTE, 1973; Hunter, 1974)
- An education free of inherited biases, with freedom to explore other perspectives and cultures, inspired by the goal of making children sensitive to the plurality of the ways of life, different modes of analyzing experiences and ideas, and ways of looking at history found throughout the world
- A humanistic concept based on the strength of diversity, human rights, social justice, and alternative lifestyles for all people, it is necessary for a quality education and includes all efforts to make the full range of cultures available to students; it views a culturally pluralistic society as a positive force and welcomes differences as vehicles for better understanding the global society
- An approach to teaching and learning based upon democratic values that foster cultural pluralism; in its most comprehensive form, it is a commitment to achieving educational equality, developing curricula that builds understanding about ethnic groups, and combatting oppressive practices (Bennett, 1990)
- A type of education that is concerned with various groups in American society that are victims of discrimination and assaults because of their unique cultural characteristics (ethnic, racial,

linguistic, gender, etc.); it includes studying such key concepts as prejudice, identity, conflicts, and alienation, and modifying school practices and policies to reflect an appreciation for ethnic diversity in the United States (Banks, 1977)

- Acquiring knowledge about various groups and organizations that oppose oppression and exploitation by studying the artifacts and ideas that emanate from their efforts (Sizemore, 1981)
- Policies and practices that show respect for cultural diversity through educational philosophy, staffing composition and hierarchy, instructional materials, curricula, and evaluation procedures (Frazier, 1977; Grant, 1977)
- Comprehensive school reform and basic education for all students that challenges all forms of discrimination, permeates instruction and interpersonal relations in the classroom, and advances the democratic principles of social justice (Nieto, 1992)

These various definitions contain several points in common. Advocates agree that the content of multicultural education programs should include ethnic identities, cultural pluralism, unequal distribution of resources and opportunities, and other sociopolitical problems stemming from long histories of oppression. They believe that, at best, multicultural education is a philosophy, a methodology for educational reform, and a set of specific content areas within instructional programs. Multicultural education means learning about, preparing for, and celebrating cultural diversity,or learning to be bicultural. And it requires changes in school programs, policies, and practices.

Multiculturalists explicitly value diversity and agree that the specific content, structures, and practices employed in achieving multicultural education will differ depending on the setting. Therefore, it is useful for educators to develop their own definitions of multicultural education, within the general boundaries outlined above, to fit their specific needs, rather than imposing a universal structure to implement multicultural education.

Multiculturalists also agree that multicultural education has implications for decisionmaking that will affect operations at all levels of education, including instruction, administration, governance, counseling, program planning, performance appraisal, and school climate. Thus, everyone involved must play an active role in implementing multicultural education. Promoting diversity means acknowledging diversity, incorporating diversity into all levels, and demonstrating pride in cultural pluralism along with a sincere belief that diversity is desirable.

The actions taken in schools to adopt multicultural education should reflect the race, language, ethnicity, habits, and customs of ethnic groups throughout the global community. In order to promote a comprehensive understanding of cultural groups, we must use a variety of methods and a composite of various areas of scholarship, including the humanities, arts, social sciences, history, politics, and sciences.

To implement multicultural education fully, fundamental changes will need to be made in the conception, organization, and execution of the educational process. These changes require modifications in an educational system that has been governed with a mono-cultural orientation based on Eurocentric, middle class cultural norms. Thus, implied in the definitions given above is another concept that finds general agreement among multiculturalists: multiculturalism requires simultaneous changes on multiple levels of schooling. These changes must be deliberate, long range, ongoing, and, most important, comprehensive.

The Need for Multicultural Education

Multicultural education should become a regular part of education in the United States for three major reasons: the social realities of U.S. society, the influence of culture and ethnicity on human growth and development, and the conditions of effective teaching and learning. These reasons explain not only the need for multicultural education, but also what its content emphasis should be and how it should be taught. Each reason plays an important and unique role in establishing the justifications, parameters, and directions for multicultural education.

Social Realities

The United States is extremely culturally pluralistic, socially stratified, and racially divided. Popular news magazines, such as Time and U.S. News and World Report, often reiterate this fact. The April 9, 1990, issue of Time examined the growing percentage of people of color in the U.S. population. A November 1993 special edition of the same magazine explored the effects of immigration on the "changing face of America." Diversity of race, culture, ethnicity, social class, religion, language, and national origin is a fundamental feature of interpersonal interactions and community structures.

However, in the more formal aspects of society, such as institutional policies, practices, and power allocation, Anglocentric and middleclass cultural values predominate. The organization and government of schools provides one illustration of this condition. Most school structures and procedures are grounded in mainstream cultural conceptions of law, order, reason, and rationality. Another illustration of the predominance of Anglocentric, middleclass culture is that the significant power positions in politics and economics tend to be held by people from this cultural background. A third illustration of this predominance is the extent to which intimate relationships are established along ethnic, racial, and social lines in the United States. In forming marriage partnerships and religious affiliations (two of the most intimate contexts of interpersonal relations), United States citizens are predominantly ethnic in their choices.

Despite the pluralism of United States society, most people live in relatively isolated enclaves, away from others who are racially, socially, and culturally different. Individuals from the same ethnic groups live in close proximity to one another, creating largely single race or ethnic group geographic clusters, such as Anglo suburbs, Hispanic barrios, Chinatowns, Little Italys, and Little Japans. The population tends to be separated along economic lines, so that members of the middle, upper, and lower social classes within and across ethnic groups do not interact with one another on substantive or egalitarian levels. The divisions between these groups are increasing instead of diminishing.

Separation along racial and economic lines is pronounced in the United States even in regions that appear to have racially mixed residential areas. This mixture only appears on the surface; in reality, these apparently desegregated communities contain insulated ethnic and racial pockets. Similarly, even in many legally desegregated schools, the students tend to resegregate themselves in social interactions and friendship choices.

The relative physical isolation of ethnic groups in the United States means that individuals in these groups are much more likely to engage in qualitative interactions with people who are like themselves than with people from different ethnic groups. Interactions with people who are different are transitory and perfunctory. The absence of close and significant interactions across ethnic, social, and cultural lines may reinforce stereotypes and cause individuals to be suspicious and distrustful, even fearful, of those who are different. Multicultural education is needed to help reverse these trends and attitudes by teaching youth about culturally different groups and by providing opportunities for individuals from diverse backgrounds to learn, live, and work together.

Although laws exist to prohibit discrimination based on race, color, gender, age, and creed, the society of the United States continues to be plagued by attitudes and behaviors that are derogatory to some ethnic, cultural, and social groups, and preferential to others. Thus, unofficial inequality flourishes, manifesting itself in racism, ethnocentrism, prejudices, favoritism, discrimination, cultural appropriation, and cultural hegemony. One revealing sign of such inequality is the frequency with which racial hostilities are reported in headline news. Another is the absence of some ethnic groups, such as Native Americans and Latinos, in leadership positions, and their virtual invisibility in the national popular culture.

Many people in the United States still believe that there is a single acceptable way to live, look, and behave as an American and a human being. The standards for determining what is appropriate derive from the Eurocentric mainstream culture. Anyone who deviates from these standards is considered to be non-American; they become objects of scorn and are subjected to discrimination, being denied equal access to institutional opportunities, political rights, economic rewards, and respect for their human dignity. Multicultural education is a potential means for correcting these distortions and inequities.

The recent revival of racial hate groups such as the skinheads and neoNazis; acts of racial hostility such as racial slurs directed toward AfricanAmericans, KoreanAmericans, and MexicanAmericans; cross burnings in AfricanAmerican neighborhoods; attacks by groups of ethnic youths against other ethnic groups; and recent cases of blatant police brutality against AfricanAmericans in Los Angeles and Detroit are symptoms of the inherent social racism that prevails in United States society, where citizens have not learned to understand, respect, and value diversity. Another indication of this social deficiency is the persistence of stereotypic attitudes toward ethnic groups. In a recent study of ethnic images, Smith (1990) reports that negative perceptions of groups of color, especially AfricanAmericans and Hispanics, are common in contemporary society. These groups are still considered to be less hardworking, more violent, less intelligent, and more unpatriotic than Anglos.

Research being conducted by Margaret Beale Spencer (1984, 1985, 1988) indicates that even though AfricanAmerican children between 3 and 11 years old obtain high scores on personal self concept measures, society still shows a preference for whites and a tendency to attribute positive traits to whites, while assigning negative traits to blacks. Thus, even young students seem to have a double consciousness, because they are able to separate their personal identities and self esteem from knowledge about racial groups in society. They can simultaneously feel good about themselves and have negative attitudes toward their racial and ethnic groups.

Discrimination and racism are evident in the patterns of unemployment, imprisonment, poor health care, and educational failures, in which the numbers of individuals of color are disproportionately high. These attitudes and behaviors directly contradict the American democratic ideals of freedom, equality, and justice for everyone. They also belie the claim that significant progress is being made in correcting social inequalities. Multicultural education programs that help youths learn to value and celebrate diversity and engage in social action to institutionalize these values have the potential to help society live up to both the letter and spirit of its democratic ideals.

The widely held assumption held in the United States that American society should be a homogenized melting pot has destructive results. This assumption works to demean some segments of society and deny acceptance of diversity. Pluralism is a vital functional force in society, even though it is not supported and embraced in institutional policies and practices (e.g., in housing authorities, school districts, and city government) and in the habits of communities. Many culturally different individuals and groups have stopped trying to deny their ethnicity for the sake of being accepted unconditionally into mainstream society. They now insist that there is no inherent contradiction between allegiance to their own ethnic and cultural heritages and being an American. Instead, these dual identities are complementary and should be respected and promoted.

One of the most distinctive and salient traits of the United States is the way in which its incredible diversity has been fashioned into a unique culture that is a mosaic or synergy of elements from many cultures. Ethnic and cultural pluralism is an ever present influence in all aspects of American history, life, and culture. No significant event in the historical and contemporary development of the country has occurred without some kind of ethnic influence and contribution. This vitalizing presence is evident in science and technology, economics and politics, art and literature, business and industry, entertainment and recreation, and popular culture. If one of the primary functions of schooling is to transmit the socio cultural legacy of the nation to its young citizens, then our educational system must incorporate multiculturalism as a persistent and routine component of programs and practices.

The increasing ethnic diversity of the United States population makes multicultural education for all students an imperative, particularly if education is to fulfill its basic functions by being personally meaningful, socially relevant, culturally accurate, and pedagogically sound.

Demographic analyses of the population distribution of U.S. citizens indicate that Hispanics and AfricanAmericans account for the highest percentage of population growth.

The total population of students of color grew between 1980 and 1988 to almost 30 percent, compared to 24 percent in the 1970s (U.S. Department of Education, 1992). As with the general population, these trends are expected to continue well into the next century. The diversity of the student population is further increased by the high rate of AfricanAmerican and Hispanic youths living in poverty (45.1% and 39.3% in 1987) and the growing number of immigrant students from Latin American and Asian countries whose first languages are not English and whose home cultures are not based on a Eurocentric or Western model.

The net result of these demographic changes is that the United States is becoming a more pluralistic society than it has ever been. Diversity in education, based on ethnicity, social class, language, nonWestern national origins, economic status, cultures, and interests, is no longer a luxury or a matter of choice, it is a necessity for the survival of society. Unfortunately, while educational policies, programs, and practices that systematically ignore these demographic realities are unethical, immoral, and reprehensible, they are not technically illegal. If the principles of access and availability that are embedded in desegregation laws were extended to educational programs, then failure to make the substance of curriculum and instruction culturally pluralistic would be illegal.

As different ethnic, racial, social, and cultural groups grow in size and political significance, they will demand that social policies and programs be responsive to their particular needs and interests. Satisfying these demands will require more cultural sensitivity, "rainbow" coalitions, and pluralistically negotiated compromises. Ethnic and special interest group tensions may accelerate as a result of competition for limited resources such as jobs, housing, and political power; definitions and visions of what it means to be American will change; and there will be greater differences of opinion about the sources of the nation's present success, future potential, and most desirable images and symbols (Henry, 1990). None of these issues will be resolved without some fundamental knowledge of, sensitivity to, and respect for culturally and ethnically diverse experiences, perspectives, and peoples, and without some power sharing among these groups. Multicultural education can develop skills to meet these needs. Therefore, the wellbeing of U.S. society and education for and about cultural pluralism are inextricably linked.

Another feature of American society that underscores the importance of multicultural education is its growing involvement in global affairs, increased global interdependence, and the shifting international balance of power. Some recent examples of international developments that have direct ramifications for the continuous leadership of the United States in global affairs are the challenge to U.S. dominance of the world's marketplace by Japan, Germany, and Korea; military crises in the Middle East that affect the oil supply and reserves; the U.S. fiscal resource allocations between military and social services expenditures; governmental instability in South and Central America, which places incredible demands on U.S. military support and foreign loan capacity; famine and droughts in Africa and Asia that require U.S. support in health care and food supplies; increasing birth rates and epidemic illnesses; human rights issues around the globe; and growing foreign investments in the United States.

These developments mean that U.S. citizens must interact in different ways and under different circumstances with unfamiliar peoples at home and abroad. Successful interactions and relationships require the use of knowledge, attitudes, and skills about cultural diversity within a global context. For example, the success of U.S. international diplomacy is becoming increasingly dependent upon knowledge and principles of cultural pluralism. Multicultural education can create a foundation for effective and successful diplomacy in the global context.

Culture and Human Development

Culture shapes human behavior, attitudes, and values. Human behavior results from a process of socialization, and socialization always takes place within the context of specific cultural and ethnic environments. The basic caretaking practices of human survival are essentially the same for everyone, but their pattern, organization, and learning are specific. Hence, humans are social beings who carry within them their individual biological and psychological traits as well as the legacies of their ethnic group's historical background, collective heritage, and cultural experiences.

When educators claim that their top priority is to treat all children like human beings, regardless of ethnic identity, cultural background, or economic status, they are creating a paradox. A person's humanity cannot be isolated or divorced from his or her culture or ethnicity. One cannot be human without culture and ethnicity, and one cannot have culture and ethnicity without being human. If one does not see color, one does not really see children. Therefore, to acknowledge and respect one another, to be fully human, requires mutual understanding and appreciation based on cultural understanding.

The influences of culture and ethnicity are established early and thoroughly in the process of human growth and development, and they prevail thereafter for the remainder of one's life. Some secondary elements of culture can be modified over time and with experience, but the core features continue to be the mainstay of a person's sense of being and identity throughout life.

Deeply ingrained cultural socialization becomes problematic in education when the schooling process operates on one cultural model to the exclusion of all others, or when culturally different children are expected to set aside all their cultural habits as a condition for succeeding in school. Such a demand .is not only unreasonable, but is impossible to achieve. Attempts to comply with it may lead to cultural adaptation, marginality, alienation, and isolation. With the exception of adaptation, none of these responses is conducive to maximizing the human wellbeing and academic success of students. The incompatibilities or discontinuities between the culture of the school and those of different ethnic groups need to be major issues of analysis in making decisions about educational programs and practices that reflect and promote cultural diversity (Spindler, 1987b). These incompatibilities or discontinuities are especially important to any understanding of the aspects of human behavior that most directly affect teaching and learning, such as values orientation, interpersonal relations, communication styles, time usage, performance styles, procedural rules, and systems of problem solving and cognitive processing.

Many of the significant discontinuities that exist between mainstream culture, as displayed in school procedures, and the cultures of various ethnic groups operate on a subconscious level and without deliberate intention. The discontinuities occur when people behave naturally, because their behavior is strongly influenced by cultural conditioning. Responsible education decision making in a pluralistic society cannot result if educational leaders continue to function without being conscious of how culture shapes their own and their students' attitudes, values, and behaviors. By becoming more aware that they are products of their cultures and live within given value and symbol systems and by reflecting on this condition, educators can free themselves from the tyranny of their own cultures and free children from the damaging effects of premature, inaccurate, and prejudiced interpretations of their culturally induced behavior.

Teaching and Learning

One premise of multicultural education is that teaching and learning are cultural processes that take place in a social context. To make teaching and learning more accessible and equitable for a wide variety of students, students' cultures need to be more clearly understood. Such an understanding can be achieved by analyzing education from multiple cultural perspectives and thereby removing the blindness imposed on education by the dominant cultural experience.

Schools are microcosms of mainstream society. In their procedural norms, codes of behavior, structural arrangements, and distribution of power, privilege, and responsibility, they mirror Anglocentric cultural values. Just as classroom teachers, school administrators, and policymakers carry their cultural experiences and perspectives into their educational decisions and actions, students from various ethnic and cultural backgrounds do likewise in their learning attitudes and behaviors. The inevitable result when these different systems encounter each other in pluralistic classrooms is cultural conflict that, when not deliberately mediated, can jeopardize the effectiveness of the instructional process. Educational activities and processes that are not scrutinized for their cultural content and implications can inadvertently give preferential treatment to students whose cultural backgrounds are most like school cultural norms:

The way...in which the teacher responds to student behavior, the often subtle distinctions made between the sexes, the nature of the classroom control mechanisms, the topics and issues chosen for classroom study, the schedule of activities in terms of the amount of time devoted to particular aspects of the school day, the spatial organization of the classroom, and the rewards and punishments meted out are...culturally loaded and...transmit messages [that] reinforce certain student behaviors and discourage others.

School leaders often operate on the faulty assumption that their values, beliefs, and actions are the norm for everyone, exist beyond any cultural constraints, or are culturally neutral. They assume that their notions of what is desirable knowledge and how it can best be taught and learned are governed entirely by general principles of good pedagogy, which has nothing to do with any specific culture. This belief is far from the truth. Culture influences and shapes all dimensions of the learning and teaching processes employed in schools.

Schools are expected to serve the human needs of cultural socialization, transmission, and self perpetuation, and teach academic skills. Every action that they take is, unavoidably, culture bound. Effective understanding of the educational process in a pluralistic society such as the United States requires that teaching and learning be viewed as aspects of various cultural milieus.

Because ethnic and cultural diversity in U.S. society is not sufficiently reflected in educational decisions and practices, schools frequently become discontinuous or out of sync with the populations that they are supposed to serve. This discontinuity exists most often when schools are controlled by individuals from the dominant culture who use only their standards to guide actions, but the population that they serve does not practice similar cultural standards. The resulting dis-junctures cause students and teachers to misinterpret one another's attitudes and actions. These cultural incompatibilities are often mistaken for intellectual inabilities, and pedagogical decisions are made accordingly. Failing to understand the cultural style of some AfricanAmericans, for example, may cause teachers erroneously to conclude that these students have limited critical thinking and reasoning abilities. The reluctance of American Indian children to operate on a tightly controlled time schedule and engage in highly individualistic and competitive activities may be misinterpreted as lack of initiative, motivation, and responsibility. Consequently, educators often engage in "mis-educating practices" because of their failure to understand the cultural characteristics of their ethnically, racially, socially, and linguistically diverse students.

General theories of learning and principles of developmental psychology that educators frequently use as the bases for making instructional decisions must be operationalized in the context of culturally pluralistic school situations and student populations. Of particular significance are the field psychology principles of contiguity, similarity, and continuity; the basic idea of Maslow's hierarchy of needs, which holds that some psychological needs must be satisfied before others can be addressed; Erikson's principles of identity development; the notion that for educational experiences to be relevant they must be perceived as personally meaningful to students; the detrimental effects that stress and anxiety can have on academic efforts and achievement; and the extent to which school learning follows procedural rules and guidelines that are compatible with those that students are accustomed to in their cultural communities. Embedded in these principles is recognition of the fact that the process of learning involves more than intellectual ability and mastery of cognitive content. It also includes the psychoemotional disposition of the students and teachers, and the environmental settings or climates in which teaching and learning take place.

If students feel that the school environment is alien and hostile toward them or does not affirm and value who they are (as many students of color believe), they will not be able to concentrate as thoroughly as they might on academic tasks. The stress and anxiety that accompany this lack of support and affirmation cause their mental attention, energy, and efforts to be diffused between protecting their psyches from attack and attending to academic tasks. Thus, stress "adversely affects students' daily academic performances by reducing their willingness to persist at academic tasks and interfering with the cognitive processes involved in learning". Furthermore, learning is a high risk taking enterprise that works better when students are made to feel secure and centered in who they are and what they are already capable of doing before they are asked to take on new ventures. Psychological security and a positive feeling of selfworth are prerequisites for the more abstract need to know and learn. These are some of the ideas and agruments that under gird the theory of Afrocentricity and the efforts by some school districts such as Detroit, Milwaukee, Baltimore, and Seattle to create Afrocentric schools.

For educational experiences to be relevant to culturally different students, they must reflect and connect with the students' particular life experiences and perspectives. This need reflects the fact that learning is more effective when new ideas are related to prior knowledge and initially are taught in ways familiar to students (e.g., the principles of continuity and similarity). It evokes two other beliefs common to U.S. education philosophy: "start teaching where students are" and "expand the social, cultural, and intellectual horizons of students." These beliefs and principles require that cultural diversity be a driving force in all educational decision making, from determining students' readiness for learning to designing curricula, selecting instructional materials, appraising performance, and developing appropriate programs and teaching techniques for culturally different students. The reason, simply stated, is that students learn in different ways and under different conditions, many of which are governed by their cultural socialization.

Some of the most salient specific ideas embedded in the three general categories of assumptions about the nature of society in the United States and the relationships between culture, humanity, teaching, and learning discussed above can be summarized as follows:

- Multicultural education is a basic for all students in a culturally, ethnically, and socially pluralistic society such as the United States.
- Ethnicity and culture are influential variables in shaping individual identity and behavior.
- cultural socialization are ingrained early and deeply in the human personality and persist thereafter.
- Cultural diversity is a normative description of U.S. society.
- Multicultural education is compatible with U.S. democratic ideals and is complementary to quality education.
- Because most people in the U.S. live in ethnic and cultural enclaves, they have only tangential interactions with and superficial knowledge of people who are culturally different from themselves.
- Ethnicity, culture, and humanness are inextricably linked and interrelated.
- No one model for being American or human is equally applicable to everyone.
- Culture shapes human behavior, values, and beliefs
- Culture and ethnicity have both intrinsic worth and instrumental value for creating an effective and representative system of education that mirrors social realities in the United States and the world.
- The increasing diversification of U.S. society and persistent racial tensions heighten the need for multicultural education in all schools.
- Education decisions made without due consideration of cultural pluralism cannot serve

the needs of the greatest number of students in the best possible way.

- Application of and knowledge about cultural pluralism improve the quest for educational access, equity, and excellence for all students.
- Incompatibilities in cultural structures, procedural rules, value orientations, referent points, and performance styles may cause school failure more than intellectual ability for some culturally different students. Thus, maximizing school success requires social competence, academic capability, and cultural congruity.

Major Goals of Multicultural Education

The expected outcomes of multicultural education are embedded in its definitions, justification, and assumptions, and they exhibit some clearly discernible patterns. While specific goals and related objectives are quite numerous, and vary according to contextual factors such as school settings, audiences, timing, purposes, and perspectives, they fall into seven general clusters. They cover all three domains of learning (cognitive, affective, and action) and incorporate both the intrinsic (ends) and instrumental (means) values of multicultural education. These goal clusters are ethnic and cultural literacy, personal development, attitude and values clarification, multicultural social competence, basic skills proficiency, educational equity and excellence, and empowerment for societal reform. Each one is discussed briefly below.

Developing Ethnic and Cultural Literacy

One of the primary and persistent reasons for the movement to include cultural pluralism in school programs is to correct what advocates call "sins of omission and commission." First, we must provide students with information about the history and contributions of ethnic groups who traditionally have been excluded from instructional materials and curricula;

and second, we must replace the distorted and biased images of those groups that were included in the curricula with more accurate and significant information. These goals continue to be major concerns of multicultural education, because many students still know too little about the history, heritage, culture, and contributions of groups of color in the United States. Groups that are highly visible in the popular culture, such as AfricanAmericans and Mexican Americans, are somewhat more familiar to students than others that are smaller in number and less accessible in the public press, such as Asian Americans and Native Americans. The information about and images of ethnic group members and experiences portrayed in popular culture and mass media are often inaccurate, distorted, superficial, one dimensional, and incomplete. The prominence of AfricanAmericans in the music and professional athletics industries and their disproportionate representation in penal institutions may lead some students to conclude that the only contributions to U.S. society by these groups has been in these highly visible areas. Similarly, if students are exposed only to racist portrayals of Native Americans, which cast them as noble savages caught forever in a historical time warp, wearing skimpy clothes, feathers, and war paint, living in teepees, and riding horses bareback, they have no idea of how to place Indians accurately in contemporary times, productively engaged in the wide variety of activities that characterize human life.

The persistence of these types of caricatures about ethnic groups, coupled with restricted interethnic group interaction, reinforces the need for students to learn accurate information about ethnic groups' contributions to the history, life, and culture of the United States. Thus, a major goal of multicultural education is to learn about the historical backgrounds, languages, cultural characteristics, contributions, critical events, significant individuals, and social, political, and economic conditions of various majority and minority ethnic groups, such as

AfricanAmericans, Hispanics, Asian Americans, American Indians, and Eastern Europeans. This information should be comprehensive, analytical, and comparative, and should include similarities and differences within and among groups.

This goal is appropriate for both majority students and for those who are members of various ethnic minority groups. A mistake frequently made by educators is to assume either that members of ethnic minority groups already know their culture and history or that this kind of knowledge is relevant only to them. Multicultural education argues to the contrary. Membership in an ethnic group does not guarantee self knowledge or exclusive ownership of knowledge about that group. Acquiring knowledge about the history, life, and culture of ethnic groups is appropriate for all students because they need to learn more, with greater accuracy, about their own cultural heritages and those of others. Furthermore, knowledge about ethnic pluralism is a necessary foundation for respecting, appreciating, valuing, and celebrating diversity, both nationally and internationally.

Personal Development

The psychological underpinnings of multicultural education explain its emphasis on developing greater self understanding, positive self concepts, and pride in one's ethnic identity. Emphasizing these areas is part of multicultural education's goal of contributing to the personal development of students, which contends that a better sense of self contributes to the overall intellectual, academic, and social achievement of students. Students who feel good about themselves are likely to be more open and receptive to interaction with others and to respect their cultures and identities. This argument is further justified by claims made about the reciprocal relationship between self concept, academic achievement, ethnicity, culture, and individual identity.

Many students have internalized the negative and distorted conceptions of their own and other ethnic groups, a process that has been promoted in larger society. Students from groups of color may be convinced that their heritages have little of value to offer, while those from dominant groups may have inflated notions about their significance. Developing a better understanding of their own and other ethic groups and cultural experiences can correct these distortions. Multicultural education also helps educators to fulfill the goals of maximizing human potential, meeting individual needs, and teaching the whole child by enhancing feelings of personal worth, confidence, and competence. It creates a psychosocial state of readiness in individuals and learning environments, which has a positive effect upon academic efforts and task mastery.

Attitudes and Value Clarification

Strong ethnic prejudice and ethnocentric values persist in U.S. society, based upon and driven by beliefs that have no basis in fact, but are commonly evoked. Several examples illustrate this point. The high unemployment rates among AfricanAmericans, Puerto Ricans, Mexican Americans, and American Indians lead some people to believe that these groups are lazy and have no work ethic. The control of most major institutions and power positions by European Americans cause some people to think that these positions were acquired because European Americans have innate intellectual superiority and are destined to be leaders. The prominence of recent immigrants and racial group members in low level service jobs cause some people to conclude that their economic status is synonymous with their human worth, and to act accordingly. Asian Americans are thought to be highly intelligent because Japanese and Chinese Americans often perform well on selected measures of intellectual ability.

The tendency to ascribe attributes and behaviors of individuals to the entire ethnic group to which they belong is the basis for perpetuating stereotypes, prejudices, and racism. This tendency, along with the disparities in distribution of opportunities and rewards in American society, supports multicultural education's goal of clarifying ethnic attitudes and values. It includes confronting prejudices, stereotypes, ethnocentrism, and racism directly; critical analysis of the sources, expressions, and effects of negative ethnic attitudes and values; reconciling differences between ethnic beliefs and truth, supported by documented facts; and developing new, more positive, and enriched ethnic attitudes, beliefs, and values to replace the old, negative ones.

Multicultural education also promotes the core values that stem from the principles of human dignity, justice, equality, freedom, self determination, and democracy. The intent is to teach youths to respect and embrace ethnic pluralism, to realize that cultural differences are not synonymous with deficiencies or inferiorities, and to recognize that diversity is an integral part of the human condition and U.S. life. Clarifying ethnic attitudes and values is designed to help students understand that some conflict of values is unavoidable in ethnically and racially pluralistic societies; that conflict does not have to be corrosive and divisive, when managed well it can be a catalyst for social progress; that there is strength in ethnic and cultural pluralism; that ethnic allegiance and national loyalty are not irreconcilable; and that cooperation and coalition among ethnic groups are not dependent upon having identical beliefs, values, and behaviors. Analyzing and clarifying ethnic attitudes and values are key steps in the process of unleashing the creative potential of individuals for self renewal and of society for continuous growth and development.

Multicultural Social Competence

It is imperative that students learn how to interact with and understand people who are ethnically, racially, and culturally different from themselves. The United States and the world are becoming increasingly more diverse, compact, and interdependent. Yet, for most students, the formative years of their lives are spent in ethnically and culturally isolated or encapsulated enclaves. This existence does not adequately prepare them to function effectively in ethnically different environments and multicultural settings. Attempts at cross cultural interactions are often stymied by negative attitudes, values, and expectations; cultural blunders; and by trying to impose rules of social etiquette from one cultural system onto another. The results are often heightened interracial and interethnic group frustrations, anxiety, fears, failures, and hostilities.

Multicultural education can ease these tensions by teaching skills in cross cultural communication, interpersonal relations, perspective taking, contextual analysis, understanding alternative points of view and frames of reference, and analyzing how cultural conditions affect values, attitudes, beliefs, preferences, expectations, and behaviors. It also can help students learn how to understand cultural differences without making hasty and arbitrary value judgments about their intrinsic worth. Attaining these goals can be expedited by providing wide varieties of opportunities for students to practice their cultural competence and to interact with different ethnic peoples, experiences, and situations.

Basic Skill Proficiency

A major goal of multicultural education is to facilitate the teaching and learning of basic literacy skills of ethnically different students. Its importance evolves from the persistence and magnitude of school failure of Hispanics, AfricanAmericans, and American Indians; the relationships among relevance of instructional materials, academic efforts, and achievement; and the fact that multicultural education includes content and process, ideology and methodology. It builds on the premise that some of this failure is due to methodological or pedagogical inadequacies of schools and teaching instead of the intellectual abilities of students of color.

Multicultural education can improve mastery of reading, writing, and mathematical skills; subject matter content; and intellectual process skills such as problem solving, critical thinking, and conflict resolution by providing content and techniques that are more meaningful to the lives and frames of reference of ethnically different students. Using ethnic materials, experiences, and examples as the contexts for teaching, practicing, and demonstrating mastery of academic and subject matter skills increases the appeal of the tools of instruction, heightens the practical relevance of the skills to be learned, and improves students' time on task. This combination of conditions leads to greater focused efforts, task persistence, skill mastery, and academic achievement.

Another aspect of multicultural education that contributes directly to the attainment of higher levels of basic skills achievement is matching teaching and learning styles. Disjunctures in how different students learn in their cultural communities and how they are expected to learn in school cause much time and attention to be devoted to resolving these conflicts instead of concentrating on academic tasks. Teaching students as they are accustomed to learning minimizes these conflicts and channels more energy and effort directly into the academic tasks to be accomplished. Thus, culturally contextualized teaching for making the educational process more effective for ethnically diverse students is a fundamental principle of multicultural education.

The kinds of social climates that exist in classrooms also affect students' performances on academic tasks. This influence is particularly true for ethnic groups that consider social relationships and informal settings imperative to the learning process. When teachers respond to these needs by including ethnic symbols, images, and information in the classroom decorations, curriculum content, and interpersonal interactions, ethnic students feel validated, at ease, and have greater affiliation with the school. These feelings of personal affirmation and comfort create the backdrop of personal connectedness that is essential to students' taking ownership in learning, which, in turn, leads to more sustained attention, effort, time on task, and improved task mastery and academic achievement.

Educational Equity and Excellence

This goal of multicultural equity is closely related to the goal of basic skill mastery, but is much broader and more philosophical. It derives from the notion that educational excellence is unattainable for any student when certain groups are denied a fair chance to receive the highest quality education possible and when some contributions are systematically excluded from the U.S. and human stories. It builds upon the idea that comparability instead of sameness is the key to providing equitable educational opportunities for ethnically different students.

In order to determine what constitutes comparability of learning opportunities, educators must thoroughly understand how culture shapes learning styles, teaching behaviors, and educational decisions. They must then develop a variety of means to accomplish common learning outcomes that reflect the preferences and styles of a wide variety of groups and individuals. By giving all students more choices about how they will learn, choices that are compatible with their cultural styles, none will be unduly advantaged or disadvantaged at the procedural levels of learning. These choices will lead to closer parallelism (e.g., equity) in opportunities to learn and more comparability in students' achieving the maximum of their own intellectual capabilities (e.g., excellence). Other aspects of this goal include teaching accurate information about all segments of U.S. society; developing a sense of social consciousness, moral courage, and commitment to equality; and acquiring skills in political activism for reforming society to make it more humane, sympathetic toward cultural pluralism, morally just, and egalitarian. Therefore, the multicultural goal of achieving educational equity and excellence encompasses cognitive, affective, and behavioral skills, as well as the principles of democracy.

Chapter 4

Role of Education in Social Reform

The ultimate goal of multicultural education is to begin a process of change in schools that will ultimately extend to society. This goal will be accomplished by cultivating in students attitudes, values, habits, and skills so that they can become social change agents who are committed to reforming society in order to eradicate ethnic and racial disparities in opportunities and are willing to act upon this commitment. To do so, they need to improve their knowledge of ethnic issues as well as develop decision making abilities, social action skills, leadership capabilities, a sense of political efficacy, and a moral commitment to human dignity and equality. That is, they not only need to understand and appreciate why ethnicity and cultural pluralism are salient features of human life and U.S. society, but also how to translate this knowledge into decisions and actions related to key sociopolitical issues, events, concerns, and situations.

This goal and related skill development are designed to make society more genuinely egalitarian and more accepting of cultural pluralism. They also are intended to ensure that ethnic and cultural groups that traditionally have been victimized and excluded will become full fledged participants at all levels of society, with all of the attendant rights, privileges, and responsibilities. Multicultural education contributes directly to developing skills for democratic citizenship in the United States and the global village. This function of multiculturalism is what Banks meant by his proposal to use a social action approach to multicultural education, which teaches students how to become social critics, political activists, change agents, and competent leaders in a culturally pluralistic and ethnically diverse society and world. It is also similar to Sleeter and Grant's (1988) conception of multicultural education for social reconstruction. This approach focuses on oppression and social structure inequalities, with the intention of creating a society that better empowers and serves the needs and interests of all groups of people. It builds personal empowerment in students by establishing relevance between school learning and social living, providing practice in applying knowledge and taking action to direct their own lives, and demonstrating the power of knowledge, collaborative efforts, and political action in effecting social change.

Approaches to Multicultural Education

Advocates of multicultural education offer many different suggestions for how it can be accomplished in school practice. Christine Bennett, James Banks, Ricardo Garcia, Sonia Nieto, Geneva Gay, Christine Sleeter, Carl Grant, and Margaret Gibson are among the leaders in the field who have developed models for implementing multicultural education. These models tend to be developmental and cumulative, as well as somewhat historical in nature. They start with the simplest techniques and proceed to more complex ones. They also tend to indicate how current efforts to implement multicultural education have evolved from those that appeared when the movement began in the late 1960s. For example, Banks (1993a) identifies four approaches to multicultural education, each increasingly more significant and comprehensive: (1) teaching about contributions of culturally different groups and individuals; (2) an additive approach in which multicultural lessons and units of study are supplements or appendages to existing curricula; (3) a transformation approach in which the basic nature of curriculum and instruction are changed to reflect the perspective and experiences of diverse cultural, ethnic, racial, and social groups; and (4) a decision making and social action approach that teaches students how to clarify their ethnic and cultural values, and to engage in socio political action for greater equality, freedom, and justice for everyone.

Sleeter and Grant reviewed the published literature on multicultural education to determine how the field was being conceptualized. Their analysis generated four common approaches: (1) teaching culturally different students to fit into mainstream society; (2) a human relations approach that emphasizes diverse peoples living together harmoniously; (3) the single group studies approach, which concentrates on developing awareness, respect, and acceptance of one group at a time; (4) focusing on prejudice reduction, providing equal opportunities and social justice for all groups and the effects of inequitable power distribution on ethnic or cultural groups. To this list they added a fifth: education that is multicultural and social reconstructionist and teaches students to become analytical and critical thinkers and social reformers who are committed to redistribution of power and other resources among diverse groups.

Since other proposed approaches to multicultural education are variations on these suggestions by Banks and Grant and Sleeter, there is no need to elaborate upon them here. However, three general approaches can be extrapolated from these more specific approaches: (1) teaching content about cultural pluralism, (2) teaching culturally different students, and (3) using cultural pluralism to teach other academic subjects and intellectual skills. Teaching about cultural pluralism is the most traditional and common approach. It is primarily content centered, with an emphasis on developing units of instruction (lessons, modules, courses) about the history, heritage, contributions, and social issues of ethnic groups. These units may be designed to be included in any school subject, but most often appear in social studies, language arts, and fine arts. Another manifestation of this approach is analyzing textbooks and other instructional materials for their treatment of people of color and revising them when necessary to increase their accuracy and overall representation of cultural diversity. Regardless of the particular strategy used, teaching about cultural diversity tends to concentrate on providing more factually correct information about ethnic and cultural groups that traditionally have been underrepresented in U.S. society and educational programs or have been treated with prejudice and bias.

Teaching the culturally different is more process oriented than content oriented. Its center of attention is establishing more effective instructional relationships and rapport with students from different ethnic, cultural, and racial backgrounds as a basis for improving educational opportunities and outcomes. Teachers, administrators, counselors, and supervisors learn about the cultural values and experiences of different cultural groups to determine how they may affect attitudes and actions in teaching learning situations. The new insights gained are then used to determine the kinds of changes that are needed in the educational process to make learning opportunities for ethnically different students more comparable in kind and quality to their middleclass, Anglo counterparts.

The underlying premise of this approach to multicultural education is that an interactive relationship exists between culture and cognition, education and ethnicity, and teaching learning styles and cultural conditioning. The extent to which these concepts are made explicit in educational decision making has a significant impact on culturally different students' access to equal status knowledge. Whereas teaching about cultural pluralism emphasizes materials development and curriculum design, teaching the culturally different gives priority to teacher education, staff development, and classroom instruction. The idea behind it is that if the attitudes, values, and knowledge teachers have about culturally different students are improved, then the decisions they make and actions they take in planning and implementing programs will reflect these changes. That is, teachers will be able to provide more culturally relevant instruction for students from different ethnic, racial, and social backgrounds.

The third approach to multicultural education combines content and process, and is often referred to as infusion. In practice, it means using culturally pluralistic content, experiences, and perspectives in teaching other knowledge and skills. Ethnic and cultural materials provide the contexts for students to practice and demonstrate mastery of more general academic and subject matter skills. For example, ethnic novels, poetry, stories, and folklore are used in the process of teaching various reading skills, such as comprehension, vocabulary, and inferring meaning. Patterns of ethnic migration and settlement might be used to teach geographic directions and locations. Ethnic and gender employment trends could be used for students to practice and demonstrate such mathematical skills as ratio, percentages, proportions, and probabilities. Critical thinking, problem solving, and values analysis skills might be developed as students examine issues, events, and situations particularly germane to the historical and contemporary experiences of different groups of color and social class in the United States, such as their images and portrayals in mass media, affirmative action, economic exploitation, and political oppression. Additionally, the knowledge that teachers and other school leaders acquire about how cultural conditioning affects behavior in learning situations is employed in making decisions about what instructional strategies, performance appraisal, curricular materials, needs assessment, and learning climates are most appropriate to maximize the educational opportunities of culturally different students.

Using cultural pluralism in all teaching and learning activities as a way to implement multicultural education is based on four major premises: (1) using diversified means to achieve common learning outcomes is the best way to give culturally different students an equal chance at comparable quality educational opportunities; (2) cultural diversity is a characteristic trait of American society, and since a major function of schooling is socialization into the national culture, ethnic and cultural pluralism should be a core element of the educational process; (3) it is more pedagogically sound for the study of cultural pluralism to permeate all dimensions of the educational process, rather than being taught as a separate and isolated entity; and (4) effective multicultural education requires comprehensive efforts that integrate attitudes, values, content, and actions and involve all aspects of the education system simultaneously.

Key Principles of Multicultural Education

Multicultural education is based on some commonly asserted principles. The frequency and consistency with which these principles are declared across time and advocates are other strong indications of the consensus that exists about some essential, baseline features of multicultural education and a convincing counterargument to claims that the field lacks conceptual clarity.

A principle is a basic or essential quality that determines the intrinsic nature of something. Multicultural education includes several characteristics or traits that, as a composite, distinguish its inherent nature and quality from other educational innovations. Parekh (1986) sets the overall tone of multicultural education in his judgment that multicultural education is good education for all children. To endorse multicultural education is not to imply that the entire education system should be destroyed or that the Anglocentric cultural dominance existing in schooling should merely be replaced with the dominance of other ethnic cultures; neither is it to deny the need for a common national culture. Rather, it simply says that the education system needs to be improved by becoming less culturally monolithic, rigid, biased, hegemonic, and ethnocentric. The prevailing norm in educational decision making and operating procedures should be cultural pluralism and heterogeneity, instead of cultural hegemony or homogeneity. Asante (1991/92) captures this intent and orientation in his explanation that the goal is to achieve cultural pluralism without hierarchy.

The general principles of multicultural education are supported by several more specific ones. Multiculturalists describe the most salient "personality traits" of multicultural education as follows:

- A personally empowering, socially transformative, and pedagogically humanistic process
- Correcting and rehabilitating some of the mistakes that schools have made in educating culturally different children, especially those of color and poverty
- A search for scholarly honesty and truth by giving due recognition to the contributions of diverse groups and cultures to the collective accomplishments of humankind and the United States
- Fundamentally an affective and humanistic enterprise that aims to achieve greater understanding and appreciation of diverse cultures and peoples
- Both content and process, structure and substance, action and reflection, knowledge and values, philosophy and methodology, an educational means and an end
- For all students in all grades, subjects, and school settings
- A means of achieving parity in educational opportunities for diverse students
- A process of systematic and systemic change that is developmental, progressive, and ongoing

- A confluence of diverse cultural heritages, experiences, perspectives, and contributions
- Has inherent merit for its own sake, as well as instrumental value for facilitating other educational goals
- A bridge for making meaningful connections between the abstractions of schooling and the actual life experiences of ethnically and culturally different students
- A vehicle for and conduit of relevance, equity, excellence, and personal meaningfulness in education for culturally diverse students
- An acceptance and celebration of diversity as a normal fact of human life, U.S. society, and schooling
- A personification of the U.S. democratic ideal of equality as practiced in school programs that accept all peoples' contributions, cultures, issues, and experiences as worth educational content

Effects of Multicultural Education

Research findings that verify the conceptual claims about the effects of multicultural education are rather sparse. This relative lack of research is due largely to the nature and relative youth of the field. During the 25 or so years of multicultural education's existence, most research and scholarship have been devoted to defining the conceptual parameters of the field, documenting cultural characteristics, and developing sample curricula and instructional strategies for classroom practice. The fact that multicultural education is a very heavily affective endeavor means that it does not lend itself easily to traditional empirical research methods and paradigms. Furthermore, since the field is still emerging, defining itself, and charting its directions, much of the scholarly activities deal with various segments or components of the field rather than the field as an entity. The empirical research that does exist deals with separate segments of the field, such as self concepts, literacy, cooperative learning, and ethnic identity development.

Some of the most compelling verifications of the overall benefits of multicultural education are autobiographical and anecdotal stories that leaders in the field share among themselves in their interpersonal interactions. Invariably, they testify to the positive effect of the principles and experiences they accrued relative to their self concepts, self esteem, sense of personal confidence and competence, social and interpersonal skills, and academic performance. These benefits, however, are not readily accessible to average audiences, since they are not included in formal disseminations such as conference presentations and scholarly publications. Consequently, research findings on the effects of multicultural education are still largely preliminary, tentative, and inconclusive. Much of it deals with identifying and describing culturally pluralistic variables such as cultural values, learning styles, communication styles, and presentation/performance styles of various ethnic groups. These findings, summarized here, should be understood accordingly.

Reviews of research compiled by Banks and Gay (1991) are useful summaries for discerning the directions and trends that are emerging about the effects of multicultural education. The Banks reviews focus on modification of racial attitudes through the use of curriculum units and courses, instructional materials, reinforcements, and teaching methods. Many of these studies were conducted in the 1970s. While the results are not unequivocally conclusive, they do indicate the following:

- The racial, ethnic, and gender attitudes of students can be positively affected by curriculum and instructional interventions.
- The effects of instructional intervention on student racial, ethnic, and gender attitudes are influenced by the nature, structure, and direction of the

intervention and the characteristics of the students, teachers, school environment, and local community.

- Cooperative learning leads to more positive racial attitudes for all students, more interracial friendship choices, and academic gains for students of color (especially Hispanics and AfricanAmericans). It has no apparent effects on the academic achievement of Anglo students, since they perform about the same in cooperative and competitive learning environments. Cooperative, cross racial learning also increases student instruction, self esteem, and ability to empathize.
- To be most effective, cooperative learning experiences should engage members in common goals and equal status relationships and should allow individuals to get to know each other and be reinforced by institutional support.
- Teaching interventions that reinforce positive attributes of AfricanAmericans can reduce young black children's preferences for whites. Deliberately designed instructional intervention also can reduce prejudices toward ali group members.
- Multicultural materials, vicarious experiences, role playing, and simulations can help students develop more positive racial attitudes and perceptions. Two cases in point are "The Eye of the Storm" and "A Class Divided."

The research on cultural diversity and learning reviewed by Gay (1992) reveals some findings of particular aspects of multicultural education that were not included in the Banks review. One of the most compelling findings to emerge from the Gay review is the effects of modifying teaching styles to match the cultural characteristics and learning styles of different ethnic groups. One graphic illustration of these effects is the Kamehameha Early Education Program (KEEP). Several researchers have been documenting the effects of this language arts program for young native Hawaiian children. The results have been phenomenal. When the communication, interpersonal, and learning styles of native Hawaiian students were employed in the classroom, both their social and academic skills (including time on task, attention span, quality and quantity of participation, school attendance, reading ability, and language arts skills) improved significantly. Reading test scores increased from the 13th to the 67th percentile in four years.

Some other studies produce similar results with other ethnic groups, although the research is not as comprehensive and longitudinal as that of KEEP. With AfricanAmerican students, the research shows that their engagement in instructional activities and academic achievement improves when (1) different and frequently varied formats are used to present learning tasks; (2) activities and physical participation are routine elements of learning; (3) features of their communication styles are incorporated into the teaching process; (4) AfricanAmerican content is a part of the curriculum; and (5) the instructional materials and activities have high interest appeal. Several studies involving Native Americans in the United States and Canada indicate that when teachers adapt their instructional classroom interactional styles to approximate more closely those of the students, participation results are positive. Using cognitive frameworks (patterns of thought, frames of reference, styles of information processing, procedural rules, content materials) familiar to culturally different, poor, and female students has been shown to improve their reading skills, comprehension of learning tasks, and recall of factual information.

While findings from empirical research on the effects of multicultural education are sparse, those that do exist are very encouraging:

- Negative racial and ethnic attitudes toward others can be changed through deliberate intervention, but the process is long range.
- Establishing a closer fit between teaching style and culturally different learning styles has positive social and academic consequences.
- Alternative instructional means can be used to achieve common outcome expectations without compromising the educational standards and quality of anyone.
- Some instructional techniques are more effective than others for some members of ethnic and cultural groups.
- Instructional initiatives that work well for groups of color generally benefit Anglo students, too. However, the converse is not true. Educational interventions that are successful with Anglo students often have negative consequences for culturally different students.
- The procedures of teaching and learning are important targets of intervention for multicultural change. They are as significant as the content and substance of teaching, if not more so.
- Culturally sensitive teaching techniques that work well with diverse students appear to be effective across age, gender, school settings, and subjects.

Reform Implications

Advocates agree on some common features of multicultural education. These features provide the conceptual directions and parameters of reform initiatives for implementation of multicultural education in school practice. Effective multicultural education (1) requires total school reform; (2) is for all students in all grades and subjects; (3) involves acquiring knowledge, clarifying attitudes and values, and developing social actions and skills about ethnic and cultural pluralism; and (4) includes recognizing, accepting, and celebrating diversity as a fundamental fact and salient feature in human life, U.S. society, and world communities.

These conditions are necessary if schools are to prepare all students for the realities of living in a racially, ethnically, socially, and culturally pluralistic world, and to become change agents to transform society so that it will be more humane, egalitarian, and openly receptive to pluralism of all kinds. In content, spirit, intent, and emphasis, multicultural education is highly compatible with the democratic ideals of the United States, principles of good pedagogy, and conceptions of educational equity. It has both intrinsic and instrumental value for improving the overall quality, relevance, and effectiveness of education in the United States for all students.

The following are more specific instructional messages gleaned from this synthesis for multicultural education summarized above:

- Efforts undertaken to implement multicultural education should be developmentally appropriate for the teachers, students, subjects, and school community contexts.
- Multiple techniques are required to make multicultural education effective.
- Both the content and processes of education should be changed to reflect cultural diversity.
- Efforts for change need to be targeted for specific dimensions of the educational enterprise and guided by deliberate and intentional purposes and activities.
- Students and teachers should be allowed to engage in the process of reform at multiple levels and in various ways.
- Cooperative learning efforts that engage culturally diverse students in equal status interactions and relationships should be a common feature of reform initiatives.

- Teaching styles should be modified to incorporate sensitivity to a wider variety of learning styles.
- Diverse formats of classroom organizations and activity structures should be frequently used to allow for variability, active participation, and novelty in learning.
- A conceptual orientation to multicultural education should be selected or developed to use as a guideline for determining appropriate action strategies and as a yardstick to determine progress.

Much remains to be done before the promise and potential of multicultural education are fully realized. Its theoretical conceptualization is progressing nicely. School practice and establishing the effects of multicultural education are not nearly as advanced. Both of these steps offer numerous challenges and opportunities for committed education to make a difference. Many action and research possibilities are embedded in the theory of multicultural education. Their potential is virtually limitless on many different levels as a way to reform U.S. education; as a means of renewing and revitalizing society; as a mechanism for making democratic ideals more meaningful in a culturally pluralistic societal context; and as a tool for making education more effective for culturally different students. The question now is whether we have the courage and will to rise to the challenge and embrace the invitation to transform U.S. education so that it really does serve the needs of all children.

Chapter 5

Concepts of Urbanization

Urban sociology is the sociological study of the various statistics among the population in cities. Chiefly the study of urban areas where industrial, commercial and residential zones converge. This practice sheds light on the influence of the city scape environment in burghal areas of poverty in response to several different languages, a low quality of life, several different ethnic groups and a low standard of police guardianship that all amount to social disorganization.

There are many areas of study in urban sociology. Among them population, geopolitics, economics etc.

The Chicago School is a major influence in the study of urban sociology. Despite having studied cities in the early 20th century, the Chicago School is still recognized as important. Many of their findings have been refined or rejected, but the lasting impact of the Chicago School can still be found in today's teachings.

Urbanization is the expansion of a city or metropolitan area, namely the proportion of total population or area in urban localities or areas (cities and towns), or the increase of this proportion over time. It can thus represent a level of urban population relative to total population of the area, or the rate at which the urban proportion is increasing. Both can be expressed in percentage terms, the rate of change expressed as a percentage per year, decade or period between censuses.

For instance, the United States or United Kingdom have a far higher urbanization level than China, India or Nigeria, but a far slower annual urbanization rate, since much less of the population is living in a rural area while in the process of moving to the city.

The rate of urbanization over time is distinct from the rate of urban growth, which is the rate at which the urban population or area increases in a given period relative to its own size at the start of that period. The urbanization rate represents the increase in the proportion of the urban population over the period.

In terms of a geographical place, urbanization means increased spatial scale and/or density of settlement and/or business and other activities in the area over time. The process could occur either as natural expansion of the existing population (usually not a major factor since urban reproduction tends to be lower than rural), the transformation of peripheral population from rural to urban, incoming migration, or a combination of these.

In either case, urbanization has profound effects on the ecology of a region and on its economy. Urban sociology also observes that people's psychology and lifestyles change in an urban environment.

The increase in spatial scale is often called "urban sprawl". It is frequently used as a derogatory term by opponents of large-scale urban peripheral expansion especially for low-density urban development on or beyond the city fringe. Sprawl is considered unsightly and undesirable by those critics, who point also to diseconomies in travel time and service provision and the danger of social polarisation through suburbanites' remoteness from inner-city problems.

Economic effects

The most striking immediate change accompanying urbanization is the rapid change in the prevailing character of local livelihoods as agriculture or more traditional local services and small-scale industry give way to modern industry and urban and related commerce, with the city drawing on the resources of an ever-widening area for its own sustenance and goods to be traded or processed into manufactures.

Research in urban ecology finds that larger cities provide more specialized goods and services to the local market and surrounding areas, function as a transportation and wholesale hub for smaller places, and accumulate more capital, financial service provision, and an educated labor force, as well as often concentrating administrative functions for the area in which they lie. This relation among places of different sizes is called the urban hierarchy.

As cities develop, effects can include a dramatic increase in rents, often pricing the local working class out of the market, including such functionaries as employees of the local municipalities. Supermarkets and schools sometimes relocate or close down owing to the same financial pressure. Dramatic increases in land values also encourage further development, and may bring an increased tax revenue for local government.

In order to mitigate the problems of city growth, certain policies such as zoning or growth control or creation of an urban growth boundary are put in place, although the eventual effect of those policies sometimes turn out to be inflated land and housing prices due to a restricted supply.

Ecological and environmental effects

A major issue facing large cities is the disposal of the ever-growing volume of waste which accompanies increased affluence and reliance on purchased goods. Apart from the unsightliness of disposal sites, harmful synthetic materials in packaging, household appliances or machinery may threaten neighboring rural areas or water sources. Though municipal authorities are trying to address the problem, its rapid growth threatens to outstrip the resources of developing countries.

Urbanization often brings people into contact with wildlife such as deer (often hunting is not permitted in settled areas, and deer become quite tame), and puma, a natural predator of deer and pets such as dogs and cats. As the puma become at home in the urban setting they sometimes turn to people too as a source of food.

Increases in the size of urban areas can have significant impacts on local air sheds and watersheds.

With urban areas sprawling outward from the city core, where the majority of economic activity often occurs, people need to travel greater distances to offices and markets in the core: conversely, people in inner-city areas need to travel further to escape the city. The travel mode most often used is the car, which can pollute the air with emissions and can pollute waterways with auto fluids, grime, rubber and metal, and road salts.

Often new urban areas are built in areas where the natural water cycle once occurred, such as forests, meadows or wetlands. This can harm the recharging of the groundwater table, and can affect local bodies of water. The natural water cycle is disrupted, and often, new pollutants such as pesticides can create problems for the ecology of an area.

Conversely, while urban air is often more polluted than suburban or rural air, concentrating a population in a relatively small area can reduce the average amount of travel, and thus reduce transport-related pollution. Similarly, city-dwellers occupy less space per household than suburbanites, and use less fresh water, fertilizer, and herbicides (because they have smaller lawns and gardens, if any).

Psychological Effects and Urban Lifestyle

In the field of urban sociology, the effect of urbanization on mentality and life style has been a subject of research and debate. A general consensus hardly exists, though the differing views are closely related to one another. Following are some examples. Georg Simmel, a pioneer in German sociology and urban sociology, suggests that the increased concentration and diversity of people and ongoing activities in cities put urbanites under stress (a cognitive overload). This is considered the major cause of urban mentality - detachment from others, self-centeredness, and a rational, calculating mind.

Another well-known view is the subcultural theory of urbanism of Claude Fischer. He asserts that many different subcultural groups are formed in urban areas, and residents tend to choose a limited number of them to participate, as opposed to freely floating one from another. Some of those groups are quite informal and residents may be strongly engaged, having a similar experience to the close relationship found in community.

The escalating rise in obesity as a public health problem in developing and developed countries has been ascribed by some researchers to the rise of urban sprawl. It is believed that suburbanites rely on takeaway, high calorie food rather than on cooking at home, and that they have less opportunity for walking, cycling and other exercise due to the car-oriented grids of many suburban communities. Some suburban planners have attempted to change this, but few of these attempts have been successful.

Within developing countries urbanization of rural areas causes disruption of the social fabric. People are no longer able to practice traditional lively hood skills such as agriculture and they either have to be retrained to work in other industries or supported by society in some way. This is the case in China, where changes in education provision are required, in order to retrain relocated workers.

Changing form of urbanization

There are different forms of urbanization, or concentration of human activities, settlements, and social infrastructures. Some suggest that the dominant form of urbanization has been changing over time.

Traditional urbanization exhibits a concentration of human activities and settlements around the downtown area. When the residential area shifts outward, this is called suburbanization. A number of researchers and writers suggest that suburbanization has gone so far to form new points of concentration outside the downtown. This networked, poly-centric form of concentration is considered by some an emerging pattern of urbanization. It is called variously exurbia, edge city, network city, or postmodern city. Los Angeles is the best-known example of this type of urbanization.

Urbanization of Education

"Population issues have drawn attention since the times of Aristotle, Plato and Confucius, but quantitative techniques were applied to such scholarly speculation only in the 18th century" (Samuel). This is an important issue because the rate of population growth is a major concern. Rapid population growth is normally unfavorable because of its "perceived negative impact on resources, the environment, capital accumulation and employment among other arguments" (Samuel). Many have studied solutions to safely and morally reduce the birth rate worldwide. Population growth is slowing down in most parts of the world. This slow down is due in part to declining birth rates. Some of the suggested reasons for falling birth rates are: (1) better education, (2) urbanization, (3) better health care/health education (4) higher income, (5) labor force status, (6) status of women and marrying later.

This study examines the theory that increased education and urbanization leads to reduced birth rates in less developed countries. When women are better educated they tend to have less children. "The variable with the greatest impact on fertility is education, especially of females. It widens horizons, sparks hope, changes status concepts, loosens tradition, and reduces infant mortality. Many studies show that education reduces fertility and raises child survival, income, marriage age, and family planning acceptance".

Education is used in a broad sense. It does not necessarily mean the traditional, formal education. Formal education is important and helpful, but not the only means of education. Non-formal education is learning that takes place outside of schools. These programs are usually "shorter and narrowly focused." They can teach a variety of subjects and skills from contraception to literacy. Finally, informal education is on the job training through experience (Gillis 255). All of these forms are helpful in reducing the birth rate. "The 1990 World Conference on Education for All focused global attention on the need to invest more resources in education, especially basic education. The consensus reached there emphasized that 'learning begins at birth,' and recognized that the formal primary education system must be the main vehicle, but insisted that non formal education and literacy programs are indispensable supplements" (Thornley & Williams). This further illustrates the importance and great need for improved education.

Urbanization is the second part of this study. Countries that have a higher percent of the population living in urban areas have lower birth rates. "Urbanization is in turn a prerequisite for declining birth rates". The link between urbanization and education is that most city areas are more likely to have schools than do rural areas. Therefore, urbanized areas are more likely to have better access to education, thus contributing to a lower birth rate. Other factors such as health care and a greater income are also more likely in urban areas, making birth rates lower.

Methodology

Decreasing birth rates are a function of education and urbanization. Several variables were used to test this hypothesis. Forty-one countries were chosen from a list of countries with low to medium levels of gross national products. For each country data was obtained in the following areas: secondary female school enrollment, adult female illiteracy rate (aged fifteen and above), fertility rate, and infant mortality rate (per one thousand live births). The sources used were: The Illustrated Book of World Rankings 1997, World Development Indicators, the World Development Indicators web-site and several articles on the web describing similar studies on education and urbanization. The year tested was 1997. Scatter plots, regression equations, and mixed regression equations were the means of statistical analysis used. The dependant variables were the birth rate and infant mortality rate. The independent variables were urbanization, illiteracy rate, and secondary education of females.

The hypothesis was proven correct according to the graphed data. The first graph shows infant morality rate as the independent variable and the birth rate as the dependent variable. As the confidence of children surviving goes up, the likelihood of having more children declines. In other words, as the infant mortality rate rises the birth rate should rise as well, having a positive relationship between the two variables. The regression equation proves the positive correlation: Birth Rate= 1.90 + 0.0380 (IMR). Using forty degrees of freedom this is significant at the .005 level where the critical value is

2.704 and t-value was 10.36. The R-squared value indicates that 72.7% of the variation in the birth rate can be "explained by" the infant mortality rate. A very significant amount of the birth rate has to do with the infant mortality rate. This indicates that only about 27% of the variation in the birth rate is caused by other factors besides the infant mortality rate.

Infant Mortality Rate (X) Birth Rate (Y): Expect a positive relationship (graph 1)

Regression Equation	T-Value	Level of Significance	R-Squared
BR=1.90 + .0380 (IMR)	10.36	.005	72.7%

The second graph plots the female secondary education as the independent variable and the birth rate as the dependent variable. The expected result was, as education goes up the birth rate should go down, an inverse relationship between the two variables. The graph clearly proves this correct. The regression equation was in fact a negative relationship. Birth Rate= 6.46 – 0.0426 (secondary education of females). The critical value again indicates that this is statistically significant at the .005 level with a t-value of –5.55. The R-squared value indicates that 42.7% of the variation in the birth rate can be explained by the secondary education of females.

Secondary Education of Females (X) Birth Rate (Y): Expect a negative relationship (graph 2)

Regression Equation	T-Value	Level of Significance	R-Squared
BR=6.46 - .0426	-5.55	.005	42.7%

(secondary ed.)			

Since the infant mortality rate was such a large factor in determining the birth rate the third graph plots the secondary education of females against the infant mortality rate. The expected outcome was a negative relationship, as secondary education goes up the infant mortality rate should go down. This was again proven correct. The regression equation was: IMR= 109 - 0.902 (secondary education of females). This relationship was also statistically significant at the .005 level with a t-value of –5.01. The R-squared value showed that 37.6 % of the variation in the infant mortality rate is attributed to the secondary education of females.

Secondary Education of Females (X) Infant Mortality Rate (Y): Expect a negative relationship (graph 3)

Regression Equation	T-Value	Level of Significance	R-Squared
IMR=109 - .902 (secondary ed)	-5.01	.005	37.6%

The fourth graph plots the illiteracy rate of females as the independent variable and the birth rate as the dependent variable. The expected outcome was a positive relationship, as the illiteracy rate goes up the birth rate goes up as well. This was a correct assumption. The regression equation was: Birth Rate= 2.66 + 0.0466 (illiteracy). The data is statistically significant at the .005 level with a t-value of 7.06. The R-squared value shows that 55% of the variation in the birth rate can be explained by illiteracy of adult females. This further proves that as females are better educated, birth rates decline.

Illiteracy Rate (X) Birth Rate (Y): Expect a positive relationship (graph 4)

Regression Equation	T-Value	Level of Significance	R-Squared
BR=2.66 + .0466 (illiteracy)	7.06	.005	55%

The fifth graph plots the illiteracy rate as the independent variable and the infant mortality rate as the dependent variable. The infant mortality rate was used again, due to the strong relationship it has with the birth rate.

The expected outcome was a positive relationship, as the illiteracy rate goes up so does the infant mortality rate. This was a correct assumption. The regression equation was:

IMR = 25.9 + 1.05 (illiteracy). The data is statistically significant at the .005 level with a t-value of 7.08. The R-squared value indicates that 55.1% of the variation in the infant mortality rate can be explained by the female illiteracy rate.

Illiteracy Rate (X) Infant Mortality Rate (Y): Expect a positive relationship (graph 5)

Regression Equation	T-Value	Level of Significance	R-Squared
IMR= 25.9 + 1.05 (illiteracy)	7.08	.005	55.1%

The sixth graph moves from education to the effects urbanization has on the birth rate and the infant mortality rate. This graph plots urbanization as the independent variable and the birth rate as the dependent variable. As urbanization levels increase the birth rate is expected to decrease according to the hypothesis. Thus, a negative relationship was expected. The regression equation was: Birth rate= 6.09 - 0.0475 (urbanization).

This data was statistically significant and the .005 level with a t-value of –4.87. The R-squared value indicates that 36.2% of the variation in the birth rate is attributed to urbanization.

Urbanization (X) Birth Rate (Y): Expect a negative relationship (graph 6)

Regression Equation	T-Value	Level of Significance	R-Squared
BR=6.09 - .0475 (urbanization)	-4.87	.005	36.2%

The seventh graph plots urbanization levels against illiteracy. The purpose of this graph was to show the link between urbanization and education. As urbanization levels rise the illiteracy levels should drop.

Therefore the two variables should have and inverse relationship. The regression equation was: Illiteracy = 63.5 - 0.757 (urbanization). The data was again statistically significant and the .005 level with a t-value of –4.80.

The R-squared value indicated that 35.6% of the variation in the illiteracy rate is explained by urbanization levels.

Urbanization (X) Illiteracy Rate (Y): Expect a negative relationship

Regression Equation	T-Value	Level of Significance	R-Squared
Illiteracy=63.5 - .757 (urbanization)	-4.80	.005	35.6%

The final graph has the urbanization level as the independent variable and the infant mortality rate as the dependent variable.

The relationship was expected to be negative, as the urbanization level goes up the infant mortality rate should go down. This was a correct hypothesis. The regression equation was:

IMR = 109 – 1.21 (urbanization). This again was statistically significant and the .005 level with a t-value of –6.06. The R-squared value indicates that urbanization levels explain 47.2% of the variation in the infant mortality rate.

Urbanization (X) Infant Mortality Rate (Y): Expect a negative relationship (graph 8)

Regression Equation	T-Value	Level of Significance	R-Squared
IMR=109 – 1.21 (urbanization)	-6.06	.005	47.2%

After all the graphs were made a multiple regression line was calculated. The dependent variable was the birth rate and the independent variables were urbanization, infant mortality rate and secondary education of females.

The regression equation is Birth rate = 3.03 - 0.00120 (urbanization) + 0.0317 (IMR) - 0.0134 (secondary education). The data for the infant mortality rate is statistically significant at the .005 level. The secondary education of females is significant at the .025 level and urbanization is significant at the .40 level. The R-squared value indicates that urbanization, infant mortality rate and secondary education of females can explain 74.1% of the variation in the birth rate. Only about 26% are due to other factors.

Mixed Regression: Birth Rate Vs. Urbanization, IMR & Secondary Education of Females

Regression Equation	T-Value	Level of Significance	R-Squared
BR= 3.03 - .00120 (urbanization) + .0317 (IMR) - .0134 (Secondary ed)	Urbanization -.14 IMR 5.67 Secondary –2.03	.40 .005 .025	74.1%

A second mixed regression was done excluding urbanization so the secondary education of women and the infant mortality rate could be tested versus the birth rate.

The regression equation was Birth rate= 2.97 + 0.0322 (IMR) - 0.0135 (secondary education). Eliminating urbanization from the equation made the t-values of the infant mortality rate and secondary education of women increase slightly.

The R-squared value shows that the infant mortality rate and the secondary education of females explain 74.8% of the birth rate.

Mixed Regression: Birth Rate Vs. Infant Mortality Rate and Secondary Education of Females

Regression Equation	T-Value	Level of Significance	R-Squared
BR= 2.97 + .0322 (IMR) - .0135 (secondary ed)	IMR 7.12 Secondary – 2.07	.005 .025	74.8%

Although education, urbanization, and decreases in the infant mortality rate account for much of the decline in birth rate, other factors do contribute. One is health care. The more health care given to women and more focus on the infant mortality rate definitely lowers the birth rate. If couples expect the children they have to survive they will be less likely to have more. Later marriage age also helps explain why birth rates are declining. Gaining status in the labor force for females is another factor. "Research has established that female employment, especially non-agricultural, reduces fertility, as well as dependence and increases women's desire to marry later and limit births" (Samuel). The status of women as a whole is another contributor, not just in the work force. Finally, there is an inverse relationship between birth rates and gross domestic product per capita.

All of the variables tested pointed toward a relationship between education, urbanization and the birth rate. The hypothesis was proven correct from the tests. The birth rate is lower in countries with a higher percentage of people in urban areas, high education rates and low illiteracy rates. Education has more benefits than just contributing to a decreasing birth rate. The economic benefits of increased education include an increase in productivity, increased income, income equality and better income distribution. The social benefits are that people will have more skills for continued learning and are more aware of their rights ("Basic Education").

Other studies have also confirmed what this data has shown. "In developing countries, increased schooling for girls is the top reason why teen childbearing has dropped in the last 20 to 30 years. As more people migrate to urban areas, educational needs increase and some parents are seeing the benefits of keeping their daughters in school, researchers say" (Feldmann). The study also goes on to say that the more educated a woman is the more likely she will be to "delay marriage and parenthood" (Feldmann). "Around the world, delaying parenthood is seen as a key component in efforts to control global population" (Feldmann). The study further illustrates the importance of not only formal school education but family planning education as well. The United States funds an international family planning program that is serving people over the age of 20 but many also work to "help teens delay sexual activity or, if already active, to obtain birth control" (Feldmann). This, at times, becomes a problem in countries where it is customary and encouraged to marry and have children very young. So this problem is a complex one due to different cultures and customs.

Countries that want to decrease the birth rate need to implement policies that include education. Although urbanization is important, it is not as productive in lowering the birth rate as education. Offering government subsidies for education is one way to expand education. The government must also invest in schools and educational programs. Schools must have the appropriate curriculum and supplies in order to be effective. The placement of the schools must also be considered; rural areas need schools as well as urban. Any prejudice that might exist, denying females education must be done away with at once. The tests clearly show that as female education increases the birth rate decreases, making education a necessity. This is a difficult task but one that is much needed and highly beneficial in the long run.

Some interesting follow up research would be to look at other countries and different years to see if the same results would occur. Also, this study focused mainly on the secondary education of females. It would be interesting to test data using primary education of females to see if the outcome would differ. Another way to take the research would be to look at health care due to the strong relationship between the infant mortality rate and birth rate. This topic of lowering birth rates is one that is dynamic and could take several different angles.

Chapter 6

Modernization of Education

Technology is becoming increasingly advanced, bringing upon new methods of attaining information and new ways of interactive communicating, where twenty years ago were thought to be unrealistic. Its true that America is near the top when compared to the countries that are of the technologically advanced, and with that we must assure that we stay that way. The modernization of education is the incorporation of the internet into education. Everyone involved in any type of educational atmosphere will surely have many experiences using the internets capabilities. Using the internet as and educational tool can serve many important functions in the teacher-student relationship.

Breaking Communication Barriers

The internet is impacting the way teaching is conducted in schools because of the many tasks that can simplified with its use. Teachers are establishing a relationship between teaching and the internet because they can work together to provide the best possible education. Contacting students is very undemanding when the use of the internet is incorporated in school classrooms. This assisting occurs through the use of course web pages, e-mail, and mailing lists. The internet is used to support the teachers via use of online syllabus and email. Using the internet incorporated with lesson plans will continue to further itself in the academic realm. Another way that teachers use the internet for education is with distance education. An Example of this kind of teaching would be if the student takes an online course where face to face contact is very limited. Students take these courses from their home and utilize video, television and the internet.

People can use the internet to communicate at the same time, in which both parties are at their respective computer, or at different times when its convenient for the user.

Teachers can posses the ability to have a website that communicates important information as well as serves important functions. Some of those functions could be e-mail, chat rooms, a grade book, online testing or quizzing, and discussion boards. The best solution would be to incorporate both types into one to form a hybrid form of education. Online courses can be just as effective as face to face learning. "Research has typically found no significant difference in learning outcome for students in the online, distance education , versus traditional classroom settings.

The number of online courses is growing and traditional methods of teaching are becoming more integrated with the internet. Communications within an educational context have seen major changes due to technology. The ability for teachers to communicate on the internet is revolutionizing the expected style of teaching. On college campuses internet access in the class rooms is becoming more and more an issue. When trying to sell the school to incoming freshman to enroll, universities brag that their rooms are hi-tech and that on-line courses are offered. Students often prefer one method of teaching over the other, however the perks of the internet are undeniable.

The use of the internet has increased the expected work loads of students because of the its functions. With the internet increasing the capacity for students to do work, it will mean that more work can be done with more convenience, which should be a goal of all teachers. You would want your students to produce more work because when that happens, the teachers feel a sense of satisfaction seeing their students produce.

The internet basically attempts to reduce the amount of effort that is needed to complete dynamic writing projects for future English majors. An example of this would be an online dictionary or encyclopedia. The internet has revolutionized the way that people do work. At an cafe in Baltimore, numerous people drink their coffee while connecting to the internet by using a laptop and a cafe provided internet connection. They realize how important the internet is and therefore they provide their customers with that luxury. It should be the same in all schools, with regard to internet access in the class rooms. With the advancements in technology, comes a more cost effective education plan, that saves money for example postage and stamps because of e-email. Time is saved as well because travel time is cut out. The internet is improving education because it is being incorporated into lesson plans by teachers more and more. The internet is going to be the educational wonder tool of the future for teachers.

Benefits

- Online courses- found to be a considerable utility to teachers and students with the explosion in interest in the use of the web as a knowledge medium.
- The internet allows for ultimate convenience in that you are able to access educational material from you own house and at your own convenience.
- Students can reinforce what is taught in classrooms by using the internet to explore a subject on a more in depth level.
- The internet provides many functions that lead to improvements in the education system.
- E-mail- allows you to send and save letters instantly, -online notes- give the students the ability to access daily outlines. -syllabus- the course outline and what is expected are easy to access and utilize. -discussion groups- help the class with common questions or gripes about the course materials.

- Way to stay current with the educational trends that technology provides.
- A long distance, interactive medium of communication in addition to traditional methods of teaching incorporates different styles to provide an academic atmosphere.
- Act as a link between the teacher and student, and the classroom and the home. The internet connects both parties and makes it possible to communicate in a convenient way.
- The internet can be used as a self-teaching tool in which the interested party can research to find out information specific to them.
- The internet serves as a virtual library where you can access large amounts of pertinent information with quite ease.
- The internet can provide students with the ability to collaborate ideas with each other from their respective homes, which utilizes the communication abilities of the internet.
- Students like the fact the time is not as important because you can do work at you own leisure.
- With the incorporation of internet in education, forms of media can be shown and used as examples for possible discussion topics.

Education and National Cultural Integration

A major task of the nation state is to promote a large measure of cultural integration. A part of cultural integration is to inculcate a sense of identity with, and allegiance to the nation. One major vehicle for this task is called history, but is actually the way schools teach the national heritage.

The group of British and American historians who met in Williamsburg, Virginia in 1960 to discuss the American Revolution fell to discussing national bias in their respective secondary school texts. Out of this conversation came a series of committees sponsored by the historical associations of Britain and the United States. This distinguished group of historians issued a report that deserved closer scrutiny than it got. The report concluded that history in Great Britain finds its value in the contribution it makes to the development of the individual human being. A subsidiary value is recognized to be training in citizenship. In American schools, on the other hand, history is regarded "as a practical, pragmatic means of protecting and preserving the American way of life." One point to be noted about the British and the way they teach history is that, surrounded by monuments of their history, they live it regularly through ritual celebrations adorned by a royal family and troops and officials with ancient titles and equally ancient uniforms. In 1966 the British were still an ethnically homogeneous group who participated in their national myth. They did not have to teach it in school.

In grappling with the reasons for national bias in writing history, the historians conducting this study concluded that it was no longer deliberate misrepresentation: "As long as men live within national boundaries, their environment will shape their prejudices." To illustrate their point, each group developed a list of the most important dates and events of the nineteenth century and came up with a list entirely centered in their own national history.

The report lists five forms in which bias reveals itself. 1) The bias of inertia grows out of the failure of textbook writers to keep up with historical scholarship. 2) Unconscious falsification grows out of the inability of textbook writers to separate themselves from national stereotypes. The ability of movies like One, Two, Three and Those Magnificent Young Men in Their Flying Machines to evoke laughter from hackneyed national stereotypes show the difficulty in escaping unconscious falsification. 3) Bias by omission involves the selection of information. Not only is the information selected important, but also the amount of space devoted to describing episodes. American textbooks tell the stories of the battles of Yorktown and Saratoga in the American Revolution in full detail, while British textbooks give the same treatment to their victories in New York and Philadelphia.) Bias in the use of language is another way of displaying national bias. In American textbooks, German soldiers fighting for the Crown in the American Revolution are always "Hessian mercenaries" and American soldiers are "patriots."

Finally, there is bias by cumulative implication. "A textbook writer without violating the canons of truth can assign such an array of virtues to his own country that the reader is left unaware that other nations made some contribution to the world's civilization." Many American textbooks describe the French and Indian War with almost no reference to the broader conflict to which it was a sideshow. Similarly, no American textbooks give the French credit for tipping the balance in the American Revolution. Without the French navy and French troops, the battle of Yorktown would have turned out quite differently. Above all, it was French money that bought the supplies for American troops enabling them to stay in the field against the British.

The finger that points at American schools for exploiting history to create a national heritage does not point at American schools alone. Since World War II both Germany and Japan have had trouble with their national heritage because the nations that defeated them have taken a special interest in what their history textbooks say. James Reston wrote a long article in the New York Times Magazine in 1985 which described the struggle the Japanese were engaged in over revising their secondary school textbooks. Three of the problems are the Japanese invasion of China, their conduct in Korea and their attack on Pearl Harbor. Japanese history textbooks were rewritten after World War II under American supervision and they assume responsibility for beginning World War II in the Pacific as well many atrocities. Older Japanese resent this burden of responsibility for national wrongdoing. Very little twentieth century history is taught in secondary school and the Ministry of Education is trying to rewrite their history textbooks.

For example, what was referred to in China and the West as the Rape of Nanking in 1937, in which 200,000 to 300,000 people were slaughtered by Japanese troops, was rewritten to become an episode of mob confusion in which innumerable civilians and soldiers were killed. The Chinese government heard of this and other changes and lodged a heated protest. Korea and other Asian governments weighed in on the side of the Chinese and the Japanese government apologized. In 1988, Urban Lehner, a reporter for The Wall Street Journal, followed up on the same topic that was still simmering in Japan. He found that students were still learning little about the twentieth century. He also described resentment felt by some of his interviewees at the blow to national pride at having to assume the burden of guilt for war and the death and destruction accompanying it.

In time the Japanese will rewrite their textbooks using some of the techniques Billington describes. In so doing, the period from 1910 to 1945 will be smoothed out to fit the national myth.

It the meantime, however, the Japanese have found a way to get the story they want told over to Americans. For over ten years they have been hosting American elementary and secondary teachers on all expense paid trips to Japan. Following the trip, teachers continue to receive materials from the Japanese government.

Many of these teaching materials present history and economics from a Japanese perspective. One widely distributed workbook funded in large part by the Japanese explains that Japan's military invasion of China was a response to European and American insults after World War I - in essence, to racism. Another guide glosses over Japan's subjugation of Korea and Taiwan and its military occupation of China, much as Japan's own school textbooks do. The atrocities Japan committed against the Chinese, Koreans, Filipinos, Dutch, Americans, British, and others who came under Japan's control in World War II are conspicuously omitted - just as they are in Japan's own schoolbooks.

On the other hand, these texts pay substantial attention to America's role in "creating" the war in the Pacific, U.S. actions that are said to have influenced Japan's decision to attack Pearl Harbor, and Japan's perspective on America's dropping the atomic bomb on Hiroshima and Nagasaki. The way the Japanese government, which controls the education curriculum in its own country, presents much of this information is deeply disturbing. It is as if one sought to teach about Germany's role in World War II without mentioning its conquests, it brutal occupations, or the Holocaust.

The Union of Soviet Socialist Republics had the same problem as the Japanese to a greater extent. How to maintain continuity with the Russian Empire while establishing the unique character of the Revolution and the new men it created was a persisting problem. How could the terror of Joseph Stalin be explained? How could the "integration" of Latvia, Lithuania, and Estonia into the Soviet Union much after the Revolution be explained? How could the inclusion of several ethnic minorities into the Soviet orbit so that the USSR did not seem to be simply a successor to the Czarist Empire be explained? These questions were more of a challenge to history as part of the national myth making process than the Communists could manage.

The same process of selection that makes history an asset in promoting the nation as an arsenal of virtue past and an engine of future peace, happiness, and improved quality of life are applied to other school subjects. There is a body of literature critical of life in America, but little of it makes its way into elementary or secondary textbooks or curriculum. Government texts and courses describe the mechanics of American government, but rarely explain how the mechanics are made to work. Where economics is found as part of the public school curriculum, it is capitalism, pure and undiluted. Schools, then, rely heavily upon description of selected aspects of social, economic, and political life. The purpose of the selection and description is to persuade youngsters that their nation is virtuous, and dynamic. Its culture, and its political and economic systems offer the best prospects for life that can be found in the world because previous generations of relatives and other citizens have striven to make it so.

In the United States, elementary and secondary schools have enthusiastic participation by members of local communities. The history of the development of public education in the United States is one of local districts taxing themselves, and organizing and managing their own schools. Only in this century have the state and federal governments become involved in extensive funding and regulation of schools. Because parents and other citizens participate directly in policy decisions about schooling, this does not mean that the state does not control schools. In fact, through their elected or appointed representatives on school boards, local citizens are the state. Though occasionally local school boards will challenge state and federal laws and regulations, for the vast majority of time local school boards see themselves as the state in action.

In the general commotion of the late 1960's and early 1970's, there were those who challenged the notion of the United States as virtuous and the one best nation. That was, however, a chaotic aberration in the vision Americans' have of themselves. The excited waving of American flags at international sporting events, harangues on radio talk shows, and small sermons in letters to newspaper editors give evidence of the fierce hold the formal vision of America taught in schools has on Americans. Even casual observation of citizen behavior in other nations shows that Americans are not unique.

If society is a collection of institutions, the state works hard to integrate them into a nation. Thomas Hughes, in discussing technological development in the United States, says that objects such as the electric light and the automobile have evolved into technological systems.

These system builders have left their mark on modern technological society by creating technological systems of immense size that embody not only technical components but mines, factories, and organizations such as business corporations, banks, and brokerage houses. In addition, system builders established large bureaucracies of labor and white-collar workers to tend the systems.

Henry Ford was one of those who not only invented and developed automotive technology, he created the integrated assembly line that collected and moved materials. In addition, he hired, trained, and supervised the men who did the physical labor and minded the machines. He went further than that. Hughes gives him credit for coordinating a larger integrated operation:

....Ford's motor company was only a component in a greater production system, or network, which involved an even larger array of organizational, production, supply, and service activities. Besides the automobiles, this automobile production-and-use system involved physical components like the automobile, roads, and service stations, as well as people and organizations like automobile manufacturers, the suppliers of raw materials and components to the manufacturers, the unions organizing the automobile workers, the dealers selling the automobiles, the suppliers of gasoline, the operators of a network of service stations, the public authorities constructing highways, the organizations financing car purchases and numerous other organizations such as advertising agencies stimulating the market.

Since Henry Ford was involved in technological system building, the process has acquired many more participants, and has become much more complicated. Environmental interest groups have forced their way into the process, and the media, absolutely dependent upon advertising revenue, are not disinterested reporters of events affecting the systems that support them. An essential participant today is what has become the education system. Generally this term is taken to mean elementary and secondary schools, and colleges and universities. In addition to financial support for all of these levels of educational activity, the state attempts to weave them into a system by laws which support educational credentials as essential to certain types of jobs. From apprenticeship training to medical degrees the state approves regulation and accreditation of institutions. At the apprenticeship level the standard may be demonstration of job skills. For colleges and universities the standard is usually set as a curriculum of specified courses. To insure that unauthorized institutions do not slip into the process, states require licenses and certificates to be obtained. Where training and education are the requirement for the credential, candidates may also have to pass an examination. The perception of all this activity is that there is a system of institutions which meet standards and furnish society with skills and services of a high order. In addition to schools and colleges, the military invests an enormous amount of money in education and training, as do business and industrial organizations. Churches, libraries, families, all sorts of youth clubs, television, radio, newspapers, organizations with special interests (such as the environment, taxes, and peace), and political parties are simply some institutions that educate as one of their functions. Computer bulletin boards have proliferated almost exponentially, and while they cannot be considered institutions, they offer a vast array of information. In almost every case, the state, at some level, tries to intervene with regulations and standards.

Education as a function of national development is regarded almost entirely as what happens because of investment in schools and colleges. Both the state and the institutions of economic enterprise have collaborated in the work of bending the process of education to their purposes. The state has taken over the control and funding of schools and in the process has found that education itself has become a major part of the political process through which the state must navigate. Making education legible and politically acceptable to citizens has led to standardizing teaching and administrative practices, equalizing funding and treatment of students, standardizing curriculum and expectations for students, and adapting capitalism's production model to teaching. This concentration on schools and their outputs fails to capture the magnitude of the contribution of education to national development. Equally as important, we talk about the individual growth of children, but we treat them like raw material to be packaged like canned tuna.

Chapter 7

Education for International Understanding

The word "education" implies the entire process of social life by means of which individuals and social groups learn to develop consciously within, and for the benefit of, the national and international communities, the whole of their personal capacities, attitudes, aptitudes and knowledge. This process is not limited to any specific activities.

Co-operation & Peace

The terms "international understanding", "co-operation" and "peace" are to be considered as an indivisible whole based on the principle of friendly relations between peoples and States having different social and political systems and on the respect for human rights and fundamental freedoms.

In the text of this recommendation, the different connotations of these terms are sometimes gathered together in a concise expression, "international education".

"Human rights" and "fundamental freedoms" are those defined in the United Nations Charter, the Universal Declaration of Human Rights and the International Covenants on Economic, Social and Cultural Rights and on Civil and Political Rights.

- An international dimension and a global perspective in education at all levels and in all-its forms;
- Understanding and respect for all peoples, their cultures, civilizations, values and ways of life,

including domestic ethnic cultures and cultures of other nations;

- Awareness of the increasing global interdependence between peoples and nations;
- Abilities to communicate with others;
- Awareness not only of the rights but also of the duties incumbent upon individuals, social groups and nations towards each other;
- Understanding of the necessity for international solidarity and co-operation; (g) Readiness on the part of the individual to participate in solving the problems of his community, his country and the world at large.

Social Responsibility

Combining learning, training, information and action, international education should further the appropriate intellectual and emotional development of the individual. It should develop a sense of social responsibility and of solidarity with less privileged groups and should lead to observance of the principles of equality in everyday conduct.

It should also help to develop qualities, aptitudes and abilities which enable the individual to acquire a critical understanding of problems at the national and the international level; to understanding and explain facts, opinions and ideas; to work in a group; to accept and participate in free discussions; to observe the elementary rules of procedure applicable to any discussion; and to base value-judgments and decisions on a rational analysis of relevant facts and factors.

Education should stress the inadmissibility of recourse to war for purposes of expansion, aggression and domination, or to the use of force and violence for purposes of repression, and should bring every person to understand and assume his or her responsibilities for the maintenance of peace.

It should contribute to international understanding and strengthening of world peace and to the activities in the struggle against colonialism and neo-colonialism in all their forms and manifestations, and against all forms and varieties of racialism, fascism, and apartheid as well as other ideologies which breed national and racial hatred and which are contrary to the purposes of this recommendation.

Satisfaction, Stress & Principal

Principals and other school managers also strive after job satisfaction and are subject to stress experiences in their work. Furthermore, their experiences of satisfaction and stress have important consequences for the morale and effectiveness of the school organisation. Low job satisfaction and high levels of stress on their part will interfere with their effectiveness and through that undermine the effectiveness and morale of the teachers and students. As with teachers, increasing demands placed on school administrators over the last several decades have increased the amount of stress experienced.

The principal's role involves ongoing and dynamic interaction between the principal and the work situation. Adaptive behaviour on the principal's part involves finding a satisfactory balance or 'fit' between his or her own needs and resources and external demands and constraints. Stress is experienced when there is a serious and persistent 'lack of fit'.

If the principal is working under excessive stress so that his or her management effectiveness is undermined, it is likely that teachers and students will experience heightened levels of stress with damaging effects on their performance and on school morale.

From this viewpoint, stress results when external demands and constraints overwhelm the principal's personal needs and resources. Stress may be reduced by modifying and adjusting internal needs and resources to make them more adaptive, and/or by finding ways to reduce the potency of external demands and constraints.

Administrator stress results when external demands and constraints overwhelm the personal needs and resources of the administrator.

Devolution & school principal

Stress may be experienced by principals in a wide range of situations and contexts. For example, stress may be experienced when:

1 The management skills of the principal are inadequate to the task at hand, so that the work situation is unstable and minimal goals of effectiveness are not being achieved.

2 Management skills are seemingly adequate and the work situation is stable, but coping requires such massive output of cognitive and emotional effort that work becomes physically emotionally and mentally exhausting.

3 Management skills are seemingly adequate in that the work situation is stable, but the level of effectiveness does not meet the principal's very high expectations.

The management of self-needs

Basic physiological processes will be disrupted as the principal experiences emotional tension, physical tiredness and psychosomatic disorders such as headaches, high blood pressure and respiratory problems. Relationships with staff and students may become strained, leading to the withdrawal of the principal from interpersonal situations and to the breakdown of communication. The threat of failure and loss of self-esteem may come to dominate thinking and action, leading to procrastination and to decisions made more in the interests of avoiding failure than in reaching new heights of educational achievement.

In any programme of stress management for school principals it will be important to help them develop skills in their own management of self-needs. Among the skills and practices that may be used are good health practices (such as relaxation techniques, regular exercise and good nutrition), techniques for sustaining positive self-esteem and the development of interpersonal skills.

In addition to the satisfaction of personal needs, the other main factor contributing to stress is the extent to which the principal has management skills that may effectively cope with the demands of the work environment. In subsequent chapters, the skills required for the management of information, for the making of decisions and the solving of problems, for the management of people and for effective communication will be discussed. When those skills are not sufficiently well developed to cope with administrative demands, so that the school environment becomes unstable, stress in the principal, as well as in other teachers and students, is a likely result.

For the principal, stress management requires the development of skills in the management of self-needs and management skills in coping effectively with the work environment.

The management of time

Time pressures are one of the most commonly reported sources of stress. Time pressures include being frequently interrupted by telephone calls and staff members, having to participate in school activities outside of normal working hours, a work load that cannot be finished in a normal working day, coping with long meetings and having to meet paperwork deadlines. Principals need to develop skills in dealing with such time constraints--skills in establishing priorities, delegating responsibilities, controlling appointments and meetings, and the effective use of a diary or planner. All these may be learned and will give the principal more control over this important source of stress.

Management of information and decision making

A characteristic of modern society is that greater and greater amounts of information are having to be processed in shorter and shorter amounts of time. This is as true for the school administrator as it is for other professionals. It is also an important source of stress. Control of the work environment requires ready access to all relevant information about students, staff, the school community, the curriculum, latest thinking about the teaching and learning process, strategies for staff development and supervision, policies and pronouncements of the Department of Education and so on. Without effective information handling skills the principal will soon be overwhelmed by the sheer amount of information that needs to be considered. In the course of the school year the principal will need to make thousands of decisions and solve thousands of problems, all of which will depend, in important ways, upon the availability of relevant information. Many of those decisions and problem solutions will vitally affect the lives of others, staff and students alike. Having to make decisions that affect the lives of other people was one of the top three stressors identified by a sample of school principals.

Heightened levels of stress will have a disruptive effect on the principal's capacity to handle information and make decisions. Stress and anxiety make people self-preoccupied; much of their energy and attention is directed inward, to the consequences of action for their own self-feelings, so that less energy and attention are available for rational decision making. As already discussed, the principal experiencing high levels of stress and anxiety will commonly procrastinate in making decisions or may avoid making decisions altogether. When decisions are made they may reflect more the principal's need to avoid being seen as a failure than his or her judgment as to what is in the best interest of the student, staff member or school. Above all else, the decision needs to be a safe one, safe from the point of view of the principal.

Skills in establishing priorities and being decisive, in assessing payoff and risks, in making hard decisions and facing unpleasant situations are important skills for the principal. Moreover, in coping with the information needed in such decision making, the development of information handling skills and skills in the use of information technologies such as computers is essential.

Management of people

Stress was found to be associated with supervising and coordinating the tasks of many people, making decisions that affected the lives of other people, trying to resolve parent-school conflicts, handling student discipline problems, and trying to resolve differences among staff members. Relationships with superiors were also found to be a common source of stress. Here role conflicts and role ambiguities were of particular importance. In handling such stress a carefully thought out school management plan will be important, as will be the development of communication skills, conflict resolution strategies, and strategies for delegating authority and specifying role responsibilities.

The principal's roles in stress management

The principal's responsibilities in stress management apply both to stress control in their own work role and to the creation of conditions that will alleviate high levels of stress in teachers and students. As has been argued, if the principal is working under excessive stress his or her management effectiveness is undermined, it is likely that teachers and students will experience heightened levels of stress with damaging effects on their performance and school morale. Personal stress control for the principal is therefore of the utmost importance.

Promoting teacher satisfaction and school morale

The studies reviewed above indicate that teacher satisfaction is an important element influencing school morale, and that school goals and individual teacher goals go hand in hand. Management associated with high morale is likely to be participative and supportive, and to occur when motivational and communication forces are strong, interaction is warm and agreeable, decision making and goal setting are shared, control processes are collegial, and achievement is emphasized and recognised. The major management roles of the principal in planning, organising, communicating, motivating and controlling, therefore, all have important implications for school morale.

It has also been observed that teacher satisfaction is undermined by stress in teaching. Today people live in an increasingly stressful society and the public school, is a virtual "hotbed" of stress'. Teaching is an increasingly demanding and stressful occupation, making the principal's management of stress in the school an extremely important undertaking. The challenge is for the principal to help create conditions through which staff and students may obtain satisfaction from their work while keeping the level of stress under reasonable control.